Two Guys Read The Obituaries

Terrence N. Hill
Steve Chandler

Robert D. Reed Publishers • Bandon, OR

Copyright © 2006 by Terrence N. Hill & Steve Chandler

All rights reserved.

Robert D. Reed Publishers
P.O. Box 1992
Bandon, OR 97411
Phone: 541-347-9882 • Fax: -9883
E-mail: 4bobreed@msn.com
web site: www.rdrpublishers.com

Typesetter: **Barbara Kruger**
Cover Designer: **Grant Prescott**

ISBN 978-1-931741-79-4

Library of Congress Control Number 2006904316

Manufactured, typeset and printed in the United States of America

To ART HILL

Introduction

Heavy seas without a rudder

When Steve and I wrote *Two Guys Read Moby-Dick (2GRM-D)* we had no idea we were creating the quirky minor American classic the book has since clearly become. I would like to say that it was the great artistic and critical success of the first book that prompted this second book in the series. But to be honest, the book you hold in your hand was seven-eighths written before *2GRM-D* was even on press. The truth is Steve and I had simply grown fond of the "Two Guys" format and the opportunity it gave us to unload our opinions on each other. So, as *2GRM-D* was winding down we cast about for a suitable follow-up.

Both our wives independently suggested *Two Guys Read Jane Austen* (which agreement suggests we may have to do it next.) We considered (and quickly discarded) *Two Guys Read the Bible*; turned down also *Two Guys Read the Koran* (or whatever the politically-correct way of spelling it is these days) for fear of bringing down a Salman-Rushdie-like *fatwa* on our heads and being forced to accept our Pulitzers wearing false moustaches.

In the end we decided on *Two Guys Read the Obituaries* because: a) we were both avid obituaries readers anyway, and b) the overall subject of Death would allow us another foray in our intrepid exploration of The Big Themes which so impress the Nobel Prize judges. But settling on a subject did not solve all our problems. We still had to deal with the problem of expectations.

When we wrote *Two Guys Read Moby-Dick* we were winging it. It was pretty much an accident, thus excusing some of its more obvious, yet endearing, flaws. This second book, however, is a great deal more premeditated. And with premeditation obviously comes responsibility. Or at least it should.

I suppose this is the proper time to confess we lack this kind of responsible discipline. We're entering the heavy seas of *Two Guys Read the Obituaries* once again without a rudder.

There is, however, you'll be happy to hear, a general overall plan: Our correspondence will cover the calendar year 2005. Wherever we happen to be, we will each read the obituaries in whichever paper or papers we have access to at the time. And we will write each other about any subject the obituaries bring to mind.

Given this arrangement and our basic interests, we suspect the correspondence will cover (among other things): random historic events and people of the last half of the 20th century; random insignificant events in Steve's and my lives; opinions on literature and art; opinions on various sports teams and personalities; favorable comments on our wives; but perhaps most of all, the subject of the book will undoubtedly be death. How could it not be?

When I mentioned this to Steve, he enthusiastically replied: "That's why I want to do this! I love death!"

It is, of course, not surprising that two guys on hitting sixty (as we both did last year) start thinking about death. A bit of a cliché actually. And I am sure that amateur psychologists – professionals too, no doubt – will read our focus on obituaries as a way of dealing with our own ever-closer deaths. They'll see it a talismanic gesture aimed at warding off the inevitable. They might be right, of course; I don't really know that much about the intricate workings of the human mind (and am enough of a skeptic to suspect they don't either.) But frankly, as far as I can tell, my fascination with obits has to do with my fascination with obits. To me they're little mini-biographies of people who were my contemporaries.

So if I were to be a bit pretentious I might suggest that this exercise, this correspondence between us, is almost a sociological examination of the temper of our times. This would, naturally, be largely poppycock. Because the real reason we are about to launch this undertaking is as a means of continuing a conversation Steve and I have been having as friends for fifty years.

Terry Hill

New York City – December 31, 2004

1 January 2005 – Happy New Year!

Steve.

For a long time I was pretty convinced that reading the obituaries was a private, slightly guilty, pleasure. But after on occasion mentioning in conversation that I "sometimes" looked at the obits, I discovered I was not alone. It turns out quite a few people are obit fans. Why is that? I mean in the abstract doesn't it seem kind of ghoulish?

In the last week or so we have all been horrified as the tsunami news came in from the Indian Ocean region – over 100,000 deaths. It's beyond our comprehension. In fact it's almost impossible to relate to it as anything other than a number. Did you feel any less horrified on the second day when they announced the number at only 70,000 dead? And yet in the face of that news, on the morning the front page of the *New York Times* announced the over-100,000 number, I spent most of my time reading the full (quite long) obituary of Susan Sontag, which also made the front page. At first blush, doesn't it seem as if something is seriously out of whack here? That there's no proper sense of proportion? It's a hundred thousand deaths versus one. Why did I spend most of my time reading about the one?

I think the answer to that is also the answer to why so many people are fascinated by the obits. Because while the tsunami story is about death, the Susan Sontag obit is a celebration of life. I believe that at some level we read the obits for clues to the meaning of life. By contrast, it seems almost impossible to make any sense of a hundred thousand deaths in a matter of minutes.

I feel very out of character starting this book off with this "life-affirming" thought. I feel like such a philosophical Pollyanna, such a mainstream cliché. Like one of those people who never uses the verb "die," always euphemizing it instead with the word "pass." In my world Susan Sontag dies; Peyton Manning passes. I prefer to see myself as a wry and waspy (as opposed to WASPy, though I suppose I'm that too) commentator on the passing parade. I'd rather start this whole thing off with something less pretentious, more accessible, like the death of a utility infielder for instance.

Well, this morning's *Times* didn't offer up a utility infielder. It did however record the death of "Ken Burkhart – Umpire." It's a short obit, which talks about a controversial call he made in the 1970 World Series. (Frankly I don't remember the incident.) But what I found interesting was that Ken had earlier been a player in the major leagues, compiling a 27-20 record as a pitcher in five seasons with the Cardinals and the Reds. Why had I never heard of this guy?

I looked him up in the *Baseball Encyclopedia* and found my answer. His career was from 1945 to 1949, ending just a year before I started following baseball closely. In 1945, his rookie year with St. Louis, Burkhart was 19-8 with a 2.90 ERA. Doesn't that sound as if he was on his way to a Hall of Fame career? Apparently he injured his elbow after that and was never the same. The following year, for instance, the Cardinals were in the World Series and Burkhart didn't make a single appearance. I wonder if they still gave him a ring?

Anyway, the thing that most struck me about his record was that during his major league career he hit one home run. Curiously that is *exactly* one home run more than I had in the majors. What would I trade to be tied with him?

I wonder if as Ken died he was thinking about that day in '48 when he circled the bases with a grin on his face. I'll tell you that's what I would have been doing.

⟢————⟣

The great thing about the five obits in the *Times* today is the ages of the deaths: 76, 80, 89 (Burkhart), 95 and 98. That makes the average age 87.6. Subtract 60 and I figure I've got another 27 years to go. I've been happy all day.

t.

Gilbert, Arizona, 2 Jan. 2005

Terry,

I used to read Sontag a lot in my radical left days. I loved her because she was bright and depressing. She managed to die just in time to miss being written about by us. Obviously she had heard about our book. I'm tempted to write about her anyway, but I know we agreed to stick to 2005 calendar year obits so I'll honor that.

Have you ever heard of *Morituri*? A great Brando movie, also with Yul Brynner. The title in Latin means: "to those who are about to die!" Fair warning. Morituri! If you plan to die in 2005, morituri! You will be written about. Or worse, NOT!

When you looked at the average age of death in yesterday's obits and said, "That makes the average age 87.6. Subtract 60 and I figure I've got another 27 years to go. I've been happy all day." I know you were half kidding, which maybe means you were only half happy.

That's the thing about death. No one is promised tomorrow. Sure you could live 27 more years (I hope so). But you could have just 27 *days* to go! Or 27 minutes: "He turned away from the obituary page, complained of a headache, settled down on the couch, and 27 minutes later he was dead."

I don't say this to be offensive, I say it to give you life! That's what death does, I believe. I think you were not at all "mainstream" in your saying that obituaries were fascinating because they celebrated the meaning of the person's life, like a game's wrap-up. That's not mainstream, that's spiritually enlightened.

Because most mainstream people think death is a "touchy" and "negative" subject, and upon hearing that you or I read the obituaries every day, shrink back, make themselves another, stronger drink and meld into a different segment of the party.

I love what television star Michael Landon said about life … no, death … (you see! You can't really have one without the other.

I didn't know whether to type "life" or "death" as the subject of what Michael Landon said! Because I couldn't separate them! One defines the other. You can't have day without night, sleep without awake, and on and on.) So Michael Landon got cancer, was given a few months to live, and bravely took his final months public and I remember this quote he made before he died because I saved it. "Somebody should tell us," said Landon, "right at the start of our lives, that we are dying. Then we might live to the limit, every minute of every day. Do it! I say. Whatever you want to do, do it now! There are only so many tomorrows."

steve.

PS. Let me know your travel plans.

3 January 2005 – New York

Steve.

We are off for Mexico on January 22nd. We'll be in Sayulita, a small town on the Pacific north of Puerto Vallarta, for a week or so and then we're off to San Miguel de Allende again for three months through the end of April.

This means that we will miss the first month of the baseball season, but on our return, I fully expect the ugliest man in baseball to be leading the American League in wins, Ks and ERA. I know you'd still rather have him in the National League with Arizona, but now that he's a Yankee, I'm now looking for him to break Clemens' record for the oldest man to win the Cy Young Award. *[For those of you who are not afflicted by the illness of following baseball, let me assure you that Randy Johnson IS the ugliest man in baseball. But, at the same time, one very impressive pitcher. TNH]*

By the way, before we let Susan Sontag slide away, I Googled her after your last letter and discovered that on September 7th of 1986 she wrote a brief story for the *New York Times* in which she quoted me! Now I'm not saying she got *all* her ideas from me, but I think this pretty clearly indicates I was a big influence.

t.

3 January 2005 – Gilbert, AZ

terry.

There you go to Mexico again, but Mexico is perfect! They celebrate the Day of the Dead. That will put you in the right spiritual frame of mind for the book which I'm getting very excited about by the way.

If I had known Susan Sontag was quoting you I'd have given you a lot more respect in those years. Please accept my apologies.

I know we want to keep this correspondence light and breezy, but what if we also write America's great book on Life and Death! We will explain death for the first time. I also think we should answer such questions as, "Where do you go after you die?" Our readers will want to know.

steve.

3 January 2005 – New York

s.

Yes, Mexico celebrates the Day of the Dead, but it is in November. We'll miss it. However, we will still catch the full barrage of death cult totems the Mexicans are so attached to – all those skeletons dancing and playing music.

t.

3 January 2005 – NYC

terry,

Yes, the Mexicans were way out ahead of Jerry Garcia on death totems. And one of those totems might make a nice book cover, no? Verdad? So keep an eye out.

s.

4 Jan 2005 Gilbert AZ

Dear Terry,

Obituaries are a celebration of someone's life, to be sure, but they offer another allure too: they are often (we hope) a clue to why people die. Especially why they die young. Don't we want to know that? So far most of the deaths listed this year in the *NYTimes* obit page are people in their 80s and 90s. Today comes someone at age 46.

The *Times* reported that Steven Parrino, a 46-year-old, was "an Artist and Musician in a Punk Mode."

You hate to judge people and jump to conclusions. But as I read of the death of Mr. Parrino, there are things that jump out at me. Clues? Maybe not. Perhaps I'm being quick to conclude things:

1) He was "an artist and musician who imbued abstract work in several mediums with a relentless if oddly energetic punk nihilism." Energetic is one thing, but isn't "oddly energetic" suggestive of something else? And then the punk nihilism. Nihilism means nothing-ism. Nothing to live for? I don't know. Subconscious? We search for clues:

2) "Mr. Parrino was returning from a New Year's Eve party in Williamsburg when he apparently lost control of his motorcycle and was thrown to the pavement." Two red flags there: a New

Year's Eve party, and losing control of his motorcycle with no other vehicle involved.

3) "In addition to painting, Mr. Parrino exhibited painted environments that involved monochrome walls pounded with sledgehammers." Or would pounding a wall with sledgehammers for art not make you less likely to leave a long peaceful life? Maybe that's not a clue. It's just that any time I've ever let my mind drift to thoughts of my doing some art, I have never thought about pounding monochrome walls with sledgehammers. As my medium. Maybe I'm narrow.

But Grandma Moses painted softly with a brush on canvas, and she lived to be 101. So, think what you wish about all this. This is what obits do to us. Steven Parrino could have been a beautiful, crazy genius whose Harley hit an odd patch of oil. That's what's so powerful about death: what it makes you think of.

Steve.

♱   ♱   ♱

jan 5-05 – new york

steve

Yes, I read that Parrino obit and my first thought was to wonder how many New Year's Eve champagnes he'd had. Though he hardly seemed like a champagne kind of guy, did he? He was probably drinking screwdrivers as the closest he could come to a sledgehammer.

Motorcycles are almost as bad as cars for artistic types. Remember John Gardner, the author of the *Sunlight Dialogues* and *Grendel*; and, famously, T.E. Lawrence. Dylan barely escaped being added to this list.

Cars though are obviously worse, if only because there are so many more writers and artists driving them: James Dean, Jackson Pollack, Albert Camus, Jayne Mansfield … all the giants.

Miranda suggests this book is twisting me weird. In your last letter you used the phrase "jumped to a conclusion." At the time I noted it and thought to myself that "jumped to his conclusion" would be the perfect line to use in the case of someone who committed suicide by leaping from a tall building or a bridge.

Unwisely I told Miranda about this and said that now I had to wait until there was such an obit so I could use it. She thought I was sick. I thought I was merely being a writer. Difference of opinion.

t.

gilbert, jan.9, 2005

terry

I love that. A man who jumps to his own conclusion.

Miranda is only kidding you. She knows your humor better than anyone but perhaps me. I remember when you and I were 12 or 13 years old we would always make fun of things we weren't supposed to, especially the popular, "cool" guys at school, guys everyone else looked up to. I even remember some lampooning of some of the world's most solemn religious figures, but again, I did read your intro, so I won't go there.

Which reminds me. The phrase "he lost his life" has always been curious to me. Is life really something you can lose? Because simultaneous to the "losing" of it, there is no "you" left to lose or gain anything, including life. You can lose your keys, because you are still around. Losing something requires that you still be around to experience the loss. Because a loss is not "your" loss if it can't be experienced. So how can you lose your life?

But you hear it all the time. People hang their heads and say softly and sadly, "He lost his life." No! He didn't lose his life, because at the point of death there was no "he" anymore to lose anything. His keys. His temper. His life. Anything! So cheer up. When you die, you won't lose anything. Because you won't be there.

By the way, do you still possess your father's poems? He had a wonderful humorous short poem about death in his collection that we should include in this book.

Thanks for sending me the obit on Hank Garland, dead at 74, studio guitarist to the stars, notably Elvis. Hank played the guitar part on "Little Sister," which I think really helped make the song "hook."

"Little Sister" is an unusual Presley song in that it got re-recorded years later in country music and scored a big success. (Not many people have ever covered Elvis songs successfully. Willie Nelson did a great cover of the Elvis album cut, "You Were Always On My Mind," and Terry Stafford did a good cover of "Suspicion," but these are few and far between.) The best cover I ever heard was done when Dwight Yoakam did his country-rock version of "Little Sister" and beat the Elvis version by a country mile. I've heard him do it in concert three times now and it's even better than his single, sometimes lasting over five minutes and becoming the show-stopper in a show full of them.

It's amazing that Hank Garland lived to be 74, given that he had a car crash in 1961 that put him in a coma for months. After the crash injuries and shock treatments, he had to re-learn everything, from walking and talking to playing the guitar. A brave and beautiful life. Imagine having to re-learn all of that. We get upset at the idea of learning a function on the cell phone.

steve

☥   ☥   ☥

13 January 2005 – New York

Steve.

I don't know about this project. My problem is that every day when I read the obits I am struck by things I want to write you. I mean every day! If I gave in to these urges, we'd wind up at the end of the year with a 2000-page book. Getting it published might be a bit of a problem. So I have to rein myself in. But the temptations …

Just within the last few days there was: 1) A story on the Cy Coleman Memorial Tribute at the Majestic Theater. Coleman was a Broadway composer (*Sweet Charity*, *The Will Rogers Follies*, etc.) and I wanted to tell you about how I met his wife, and mother of his 7-year-old girl, at an art opening this past year.

Then 2) Bobby Brooks Kramer, who shamefully I'd never heard of, but *she* seems to have been pretty much the most famous woman bronco rider. She died at 91 so I don't think she was riding them much the last few years, but the obit included the information that at 90 she won a riding competition at the Billings Saddle Club.

3) An obit on Sheldon H. Kinney, an American Admiral of some note apparently. This one reminded me of the obits I used to read in the *Telegraph* when we were living in London. The *Telegraph* is rightly famous for their obituaries and has published four or five collections of them as books. They are awfully well done. But it seemed to me there were an extraordinary number of military men chronicled. Virtually every day "Taps" was being played for some Colonel or a General or some other luster of brass. Thus giving lie to the common wisdom that "old soldiers never die."

4) Another on Guy Davenport. Did you ever read him? The obit said he was best known for his short stories. Well, I've never read a single one of them, but I read two books of his essays, which I thought remarkable. The essays fell into two general classifications: brilliant and insightful; and absolute bullshit on paper. The strange thing was that I found both types fascinating.

One thing that puts me off reading any of Davenport's fiction is a line in the obit that says his gift was to bring to the short-story form "some of the lyric concision of the modern poem – *and some of its difficulty too*." That last bit reads to me like a warning light.

Anyway, while thinking about the all those old soldiers obits in the *Telegraph* (and the *London Times* too) it struck me that World War II was really the defining event for that whole generation. If it hadn't taken place, there wouldn't be all those military men's obituaries. No one would have heard of these people. It occurred to me that the categories of obituary subjects more or less define what was important to an era.

Then I said, so what would it be for our generation?

I have a couple of suggestions, based only on the first twelve days of the year. First, you probably noted that both Shirley Chisholm and James Forman got long obits in the past couple of weeks. Obviously the civil rights movement is in bold-face in our lives. I also happen to think it is the greatest triumph of our era and one of the few things in my lifetime that gives me any hope for the advancement of civilization, though I can lay claim to not the slightest bit of credit for it.

But the other category that seems to show up a lot is pop musicians. There was the one you brought up a week ago. Then this morning there were two more: Spencer Dryden of the Jefferson Airplane; and Jimmy Griffin of a group called Bread. (Ever heard of them? I haven't.) The interesting thing in the Dryden obit is that it says he joined Jefferson Airplane when he replaced Skip Spence "who went on to start another 1960's San Francisco rock group, *Moby Grape*." (Italics mine.) So there it is! That's our segue from *Two Guys Read Moby-Dick* to *Two Guys Read the Obituaries*.

Do you think we cared more about popular music than other generations? Or it is that rock-and-roll in the fifties and early sixties created such a clear line of demarcation that we were really the first – and I think, only – generation that totally had exclusive ownership of its own music? We did not really play the music of our parents, and they didn't join in playing ours (at least until later on.) But our kids, while certainly having their own groups, still listen to and like The Rolling Stones, Elvis Presley, The Beatles, Little Richard, Bob Dylan, Buddy Holly, etc. (though Pat Boone hasn't yet been able to revive his career, despite being re-born). I don't remember us spending much time listening to Bing Crosby, Frank Sinatra, Russ Columbo or the Ames Brothers, say. I do recall you having an unexplainable fondness for Louis Prima and Keely Smith, however. Also Julie London. Or was that your dad?

Enough dredging up our youth. How are your Phoenix Coyotes doing with Brett Hull? I've kind of lost interest in NHL hockey; I haven't seen a game all year.

[This was a topical joke. The NHL was at this time involved in either a player strike or an owner lock-out depending who you listened to. They hadn't played a single game in the season at this point. Soon after, they issued an obituary for the entire season. TNH]

Incidentally, yes I have my father's poems somewhere, but since all of my life is in storage because of our unsettled natures, there is no way I could lay my hands on them right now. Seriously, we've had a large portion of our possessions in storage for more than eight years now. As Miranda says, when we finally get all our stuff out it will be like Christmas.

t.

⊕   ⊕   ⊕

16 January 2005   gilbert Az

Dear Terry,

Well, I hope you find your father's poems. They were so funny.

But I'm not writing about an obituary today, but rather about a near-obituary, that of former all-pro NFL football player Barret Robbins, who was shot through the heart by police after throwing three of them around "like ragdolls" in a struggle during a burglary. He remains in critical condition.

As you read deeper into this story, you note that Robbins had reached 400 pounds, and that he'd had a history of struggles with steroids and other drugs. Will we ever know the true debilitating effect of steroids on athletes in this era? Jason Giambi suffered from a rare cancerous type of disorder that caused him to lose all his muscles and lose everything as a former Yankee slugger, and then he admitted to steroid use.

What really caught my eye was a recent report that over 65 pro wrestlers have died since 1997, mainly because of steroids. That's 65 fairly young men dying in eight years' time in one small sport? That, to me, is incredible.

It used to be that sports were good for you. In fact, it used to be that athletes had the lowest cancer rate of any profession, and since cancer is a case of oxygen not getting to a cell, you could see why that was.

Todd Bennett in *USA Today* had a recent story that quoted wrestling legend "Rowdy" Roddy Piper, 49. "I experienced what we in the profession call the silent scream of pain, drugs and loneliness," said Piper. "You're in your hotel room. You're banged up, numb and alone. You don't want to go downstairs to the bar or restaurant. The walls are breathing. You don't want to talk. Panic sets in and you start weeping. It's something all of us go through."

To me, that does not sound like fun. It does not sound like a "game" is being played.

And as to your question about my unexplainable fondness for Louis Prima and Keely Smith, and also Julie London. "Or was that your dad?" I must admit that my father introduced me to much great music from the 30s and 40s, and Kathy and I recently had the pleasure of seeing Keely Smith in Las Vegas. She still has an amazing voice, even at her advanced age; she must be in her late seventies, unlike so many other stars of her era who still performed after their voices were shot, notably Sinatra, whom I saw when he was 80. I have a theory that inactivity makes a voice go old and bad. Like any other muscle. Keely really sings a lot. The others of her era think they can just go out on stage based on their fame and if the orchestra is big enough, who cares?

S.

18 january 2005 – NYC

Steve,

Yes, the steroids thing is hideous. Remember Lyle Alzado? He was the first one I remember. At the time I think it was just a theory that the steroids caused the brain cancer, but the evidence seems to be mounting quickly. He was born five years after we were, and he's already been dead for more than twelve years. I hope he enjoyed his football career.

Obviously the whole thing scares me because, as you've probably guessed from looking at my body, I've been on 'roids since junior high.

Today's *Times* notes the deaths of two people I actually knew. Well, this is a blatant lie. But I knew people that knew them. So I knew them at one degree of separation.

The first was Suzie Frankfort, whose primary claim to a two-column obituary seems to be that she was "Friend to Warhol." I was interested to hear that because I had no idea she had any connection with Andy at all. Apparently she was mentioned 34 times in Warhol's published diaries. (I checked for your name and mine in the diaries, but neither of us made it.)

I knew of her because when I was a copywriter at Young & Rubicam in Detroit, she was the wife of the golden-boy President of the agency, a former art director named Steve Frankfort. Steve, based in New York, used to blow into Detroit when it was time to present the new advertising campaigns to Chrysler-Plymouth. So for a little over a year (which is all the longer he was able to hang on the Y&R presidency) I used to see him every few months or so in the office.

Steve Frankfort, who was divorced from Suzie in 1968, is still alive. He's a noteworthy figure in the fabled advertising glory years of the 1960s, because he was the first art director to really make it big. Prior to that time, print and radio were the dominant media and, for better or worse, the writers were the ones who controlled the creative. The rise of television in the '60s meant more emphasis on the visual, and the practice of creative people working in art director/writer teams started. Frankfort made the most of this new equality.

These days you see art directors running many creative departments and even agencies, but he was the first (that I know of, anyway). I never met Suzie, though, and now I guess it's too late.

◦━━━◦

The second was Dennis Flanagan. He's the man responsible for changing *Scientific American* from a stodgy academic journal to a magazine about science for the general reader. (And in the process increasing circulation from 40,000 to well over 600,000.) He was also a friend of my father's.

I note in the obit that he graduated from Michigan the year before my father and that he was, early in his career, involved in sports reporting for *Life* magazine, so I suspect they became friends in the sports department of the *Michigan Daily*. I don't know this for sure.

What I do remember is that at one point my father and mother came to New York for a few days for my dad to check out some employment possibilities. (Was this after the war, like 1946? Or maybe after they came back from Mexico in 1950?) They were shown around a bit by "Denny" Flanagan. He took my dad to a Giants game at the Polo Grounds, I know. But the main reason I know about this trip (and the main reason I know about Denny Flanagan) is that my mother always used to tell the story of the three of them walking around Astor Place and Denny pointing out the famous McSorley's Pub.

"You should see it inside," said Flanagan.

The difficulty was that at that time – and in fact, for another twenty-five years – women were not allowed in McSorley's. Finally Denny and my father went in for just one beer, and my mother was left standing outside looking through the dark windows like an orphan in the snow looking through a window of a happy family celebrating Christmas.

My mother – who you'll remember was not only a former actress, but also had a natural penchant for the dramatic – told this story four or five times in my hearing, always pushing the right buttons and pulling the right strings to squeeze the maximum amount of pathos and humor out of the tale. And while I'm sure the story was factually accurate, I'm also sure that hers was a pretty warped version for the benefit of an audience. In fact, I'm pretty sure my mother *insisted* that the two of them go in and have a beer while she took a little walk around the neighborhood. It's a better story her way, of course.

⸻

Reminding me of another story. This was when I was at Y&R in Detroit. The office was down on Fort Street just about three blocks from Cobo Hall, Detroit's convention center if you remember. Whenever there was a big convention in town, those of us who worked in the area would make a point of not going out for lunch because it was impossible to get in any of the nice restaurants in the area. Instead we'd order in or pick up a pre-packaged sandwich in the small shop downstairs in our office building.

One day a friend of mine popped his head in to my office and asked if I wanted to go out to lunch.

"But we'll never get in any place," I said, "there's a big convention at Cobo – nuns."

"That's why I thought we might go to the Ponchartrain Bar."

"But that's just a block from Cobo." But then the brilliance of his suggestion hit me. The Ponchartrain Bar was "men only." If you were a woman, as most nuns at the time were, all the "Hail Marys" in the world wouldn't get you in the place.

We went and it was uncrowded. I also remember it as the first time I had ever had turtle soup (add sherry to taste).

A year later, by the way, Mark Lane (a muckraking lawyer/author) was staying at the hotel and had arranged to have lunch with Jane Fonda (a muckraking actress/exercise guru). They went to the Bar and were turned away. Mark Lane said he was going to sue and at that moment the "men only" policy was changed. Do you think it was all because Jane was wild about turtle soup and sherry?

What's the superstition? Things come in threes? Today's obits featured three old-time actresses.

Or is it in twos? Did you notice another legendary rodeo star – this one a man – bit the dust a couple of days ago. And today, in addition to the actress trinity, a president of McDonald's McDied at the age of only 44. The story pointed out that it was the second McDonald's president to be served the mortality Whopper in the last year. Something's up, don't you think?

Terry.

✟   ✟   ✟

19 January 2005
Gilbert AZ

Terry,

Wow, you now know everyone who is dying. Or have some relationship to them. McLuhan was right. It's now a true global village.

But here's a question for you: Why do we slow down to look at car accidents? Don't we really want to find out what to avoid? Why do we watch bad news on TV? Don't we also read obituaries to find out how not to die so young? Don't we read them to secretly find out how much longer we can expect to live? And how people die and why?

I read in the obits today that Gene Baylos has died. He was 98 years old. (And yes it seems that people are dying older and older. Whereas maybe ten years ago I would see ages in the 70s in the obits, they are now in the 80s and 90s, are you noticing this? I mean, it seems dramatically different to me.)

Gene Baylos was a little-known comic. Alan King once called him "the comedian in residence, the court jester of the Friars Club," adding, "Put him in a room with 20 comedians and nobody gets laughs except Baylos."

The *Times* said, "Mr. Baylos got big laughs among his peers – sometimes with shtick as simple as slipping a roll into his pocket while bragging about a lucrative booking."

I read every obituary searching for clues. I want to live a long and happy life like Gene Baylos did. I want to write 30 more books in the next 30 years. That's my life's purpose. So when I read about Baylos I remember the connection between laughter and life. Norman Cousins' famous book *Anatomy of an Illness* made the connection forever between laughter and healing. Baylos was a comic and he lived to 98! Lesson learned!

Baylos is survived by his wife of 50 years, Cyrile. He continued working until September 1999, when he fell and broke a hip on the way to the Friars Club.

There's another thing. I'd love for Kathy to have many years married, and not have to say, "I married an older guy and lost him soon thereafter." She and I have 14 years together now, and how great to be able to pull a Baylos and add 38 more! That would be more married years for Kathy than Cyrile had.

But what's this thing about old people *falling*? In China they don't fall and break hips, I understand, because they all do a version of Tai Chi in the park in their eighties . . . balance actually takes practice, is the theory. You aren't born with it. How do I know? I've seen my children learn to walk. Believe me, we are not born with this thing called balance. And that's why so many old people fall and break body parts. They are out of *practice*, leading sedentary lives, not really having to balance.

So the lesson from Gene Baylos' obit is to laugh and spin around and dance and balance and do martial arts movements, or go walking, or something like Tai Chi or the more trendy Chi Gong. (I have begun to practice Chi Gong myself.)

I want to be really old and really balanced. I want to slip a roll in my pocket while telling you and Miranda how well my last book sold.

Steve.

21 jan 2005 – NYC

s.

There you are feeling all optimistic and rosy with Gene Baylos and comes today the Anti-Baylos. I told you these things come in twos. Another comic – this one only 43 years old. His car careered off a road and plunged into a ravine.

Who was this comedian? Well, Alebachew Teka.

Who? Alebachew was one of the five top (well, let's say "ten top," just to be safe) Ethiopian comics. I personally thought he was sixth or seventh best. Addis Ababa, understandably, is in deep mourning.

I suppose the lesson here is that while laughter is a key to longevity, one should not be so stupid as to travel on the Addis-Ababa-to-Jimma road.

But here's my question: Who did Alebachew know at the *New York Times*?

t.

Friday, 21 January 2005 PHX

terry,

When Fred *[Fred Knipe, a Tucson-based writer, songster and comic, is a college friend of Steve's, and later, through Steve, of mine. TNH]* lived in Ethiopia as a US Army Arab linguist, I think Fred himself, although a foreigner, was the number one comedian in the country. Proof: I wrote to him asking, How Is It Over There? and he wrote back, "It's highly selassie."

s

25 January 2005 10AM

Sayulita, Nayarit, Mexico

steve.

I was going through obituary withdrawal for a couple of days there. We left New York early on Saturday but managed to get a *Times* at the airport. And while I stand steadfast in my opinion that all obituaries are interesting, Saturday's *Times* was sent by the obituary gods to test my faith – a bunch of scientists and economists, though even then I have to say I find them much more interesting once they're dead.

Then we arrive in Sayulita. This is a small town in a beautiful location on the ocean about forty miles north of Puerto Vallarta. The key word in that last sentence is "small."

"How small *is* it, oh Wise and Paycheck-Writing One?" as Ed McMahan used to ask Johnny.

It's so small it has no paved roads, no post office, no bank, no cash machine and no obits! Well, at least no obits on Sunday and Monday, our first two days here. You see, they have no local paper, and the outside papers are flown to Puerto Vallarta and don't get out here until the following day. The Sunday papers are considered too heavy to be flown in.

So there was no new paper either Sunday or Monday. But in the meantime, Miranda got on the internet and tantalized me by telling me that on her MSN homepage, there was a "rumor" that Johnny Carson had died. Obviously Johnny's death (?) was on my mind when I mentioned the standard Carson line ("How dead *is* he?"). But as of right now, I really don't know whether he's gone or not. Though I'll find out in a few hours when we go into town for lunch; the papers will have arrived by then.

I'll write you later in the day.

Do you remember seeing the movie version of *Night of the Iguana* with Richard Burton in the role of the defrocked priest? We would have been seniors in high school then, I believe. I can't remember if we took dates or not. In fact, the thing I remember most clearly is Burton wearing a pair of Clark's desert boots in the film. Within a couple of days I had visited a shoe store and had bought a pair for myself. Wore them all through college and thought of myself as looking like Burton every time I laced up.

I guess that was a bit of a side trip. What I really wanted to say is that the place we're staying at right now reminds me of the place Ava Gardner owned in the film. Well, obviously it's not run down like hers was, but it sits high on the side of the hill in the jungle overlooking the ocean. There are 139 steps that lead steeply down to the beach. Large iguanas run around the property.

I have become in fact like a large iguana myself – sun-sodden, lazy, dusty, heavy-lidded and lost in prehistoric dreams. Of course, one can't be that lazy when you have to climb the 139 steps to get back from the beach.

t.

Jan. 26, 2005
Gilbert, AZ.

Dear Terry,

Night of the Iguana is still a great movie to rent and I do remember you and me seeing it together just after high school....everything was filmed in high-contrast black-and-white by the great Mexican cinematographer Gabriel Figueroa, and they say the movie put Puerto Vallarta on the map as a vacation destination. Here's what gets me, though. In the movie Deborah Kerr's 97-year-old poet grandfather was played by Cyril Delevanti, who was in reality only 65 at the time! But in those days 65 was just about it, age-wise. You were 65? You were older than the trees.

You could play a dead person if you had to. Today if I read an obit of someone who died at 65 I say, "What in the world happened?!?!"

steve

26.01.05
Sayulita, Nayarit, Mexico

Steve.

And so midday yesterday we walked into town where I bought the *New York Times*. Could it be they only bring in one copy? The one I bought was the only one in evidence, though I must admit we haven't run into any other New Yorkers here. (As opposed to San Miguel where there seems to be an endless supply.)

Anyway, it was confirmed: the man who gave his name to a whole line of outdoor toilets ("Here's Johnny") is dead. I must say, I always found him funny. I have never been a really regular *Tonight Show* watcher, but I used to catch it occasionally and Johnny always made me laugh. This is pretty amazing when I consider all the comics who don't make me laugh – even some that I actually consider funny.

My favorite of his characters was The Great Carnac. I remember the writers and art directors at Young and Rubicam in Detroit when I was there in the late 1960s used to make up Carnac jokes:

"And the answer is Cary Grant … Cary Grant."
OPENS THE ENVELOPE
"What did the Union soldiers do after their commander had spent a night on the town?"

That was one of mine that I remember. But it was nowhere near as good as the one I once heard Carson do – my personal favorite:

"And the answer is 9W … 9W."

OPENS THE ENVELOPE
"Do you spell your name with a V, Mr. Wagner?"

I was reading some old columns of my Dad's the other day
*[My father, Art Hill, was a writer and for ten years wrote a
regular bi-weekly column for the* Stoughton *(Wisc.)* Hub. *TNH]*
and came across his comment on Ed McMahon (you'll note that
after reading the Carson obit I managed to discover the correct
spelling of Ed's last name). He described Ed as "the world
champion at identifying which side of the bread had butter on it."
Miranda thought that was a little harsh on Ed. Maybe so, but still
pretty funny.

One of the things I thought was great – not in Carson's obituary,
but in an accompanying appreciation – was the discovery that even
after he retired, Carson continued reading the news and writing
monologue-type jokes. He had a friend he'd call and tell the jokes
to on the phone. But after a while the friend said that he should get
his stuff to Letterman. This was done privately so that it would
never give the appearance that Johnny was taking sides in the Leno-
Letterman competition.

The writer of the appreciation said Carson was excited like a
little kid when Letterman would use one of his jokes. Well, Johnny
had all the things we say you need for longevity – a kid-like
enthusiasm, laughter, no extra poundage – but I guess the smoking
got to him. (Aren't you glad you never started?) Still 79 ain't bad,
but it ain't Gene Baylos territory.

By the way, when I said these things happen in twos – Baylos
and that famous Ethiopian comic – maybe I was wrong. Maybe it
is threes. And Johnny makes three.

The other obit of note yesterday: Rose Mary Woods, who
wasn't quite as funny as Johnny. I do believe, however, she could
have given McMahon a run for his money in the buttered bread
competition. At noon tomorrow the White House in
commemoration of her passing will observe eighteen and a half
minutes of silence.

She and, I think, Bebe Rebozo were pretty much the highlights of the Nixon years. Though, I must say, Pat could be a bit of a goer when she got a few snorts in her.

Sincerely,
Terrence N. Hill – Chairman of the Baylos Admiration Society

1/26 Gilbert AZ.

t.

Some of the clips of Johnny Carson on TV in recent tribute days show him smoking, sneaking puffs when he thinks the camera is off of him, while the show is going on. So that's a serious habit, and then he dies of emphysema at 79. You say 79 ain't bad, but reading the obituaries every day as I now do, I see mostly people dying in their 80s and 90s. It looks like if you don't live till at least 89 you're some kind of loser, or there was something off kilter. Or, you were a journalist. (My informal poll shows journalists dying younger so far this year . . . journalists are stereotypically known for drinking and smoking, if the old caricatures are true.) And, again, it makes you wonder. Where do people go when they die? I asked someone that once, a wise person, and he said, "Well, where do you do go when you sleep?"

And as for your father, he has passed away, but still we can read his books and columns. So what is that on the page? Just black marks? Or is that your dad? I mean, a lot of his humor rises up from the page, and certainly his thinking rises up. So if you can encounter his fresh, original, delightful thinking in a new way, to what degree is "he" dead?

I heard Elvis singing on the radio today. Of course Elvis died long ago. (He would have been 70 this year.) Was it really Elvis I heard? Vibrations came from his voice and went on to a tape. Just as vibrations come from my voice when I call you on the phone.

If a tree falls in a forest, does it make a sound? I've always thought people were idiots for asking this question, acting like they are Zen masters to ask this question. Of course it does not make a sound. It makes a vibration. But sound is defined in the ear. You can't have sound without an ear and you can't (and don't) have a rainbow without an eye.

Some of the stars we "see" have already died out, but the light is just getting to us. By the time you "see" the tree across the street a number of the cells and most of the molecular events you are "seeing" are over with.

My point is this: death is relative. Carson can still make me laugh. I know this because I just saw an old show scene of him I'd never seen. How final is this condition we call "death" if having that condition can't stop you from still making someone laugh?

s.

ተ   ተ   ተ

28.01.2005 – Sayulita, Nayarit, Mx.

Steve.

I believe W.C. Fields said that when we die we go to Philadelphia.

When I said we were able to get the *New York Times* but it came a day late, I told a fib; sometimes it doesn't come at all. That was the case Wednesday and Thursday, but today, Friday, an old man came through the restaurant where we were having breakfast selling the *San Francisco Chronicle, The Wall Street Journal* and *The NY Times*.

I've never read the *Chronicle*'s obits so I was tempted to get it, just to see, but Miranda was having none of that. We bought the *Times*.

The average age of today's obit subjects was 100!!! Now I grant you there were only two – the architect Philip Johnson at 98 and some and a federal judge at 102 – but on the basis of today I am now making plans for the next forty years.

Another encouraging thing in the Johnson notice was a mention that he was survived by his sister who is 102.

When I moved to New York from Toronto, Johnson's "lipstick building" was new and there was a lot of comment on it pro and con – largely con as I remember. One day going past it in a cab with a client, he asked me if I had ever *really* liked any Johnson building.

At the time I could name the designer of the Eiffel Tower, but that was pretty much the sum total of my architectural knowledge, so I sort of laughed off the question. But now that I know a little about it (the key word here is "little"), I guess I kinda do like some of his buildings.

I like his AT&T building (or whatever it's called now). I like his glass house, though I'm not sure I'd want to live there (I throw stones) and I like the whole feeling of the Four Seasons restaurant. There's nothing wrong with Johnson, but on the whole, I'd rather be Wright.

t.

♰   ♰   ♰

29 jan 2005 Gilbert.

ter

I've got a puzzle for you today! And, be patient. This has EVERYTHING to do with obituaries. You have always been a bright guy. (I increase the pressure and anxiety.) So please do this exercise for me: finish this numerical sequence: what's the next number in the sequence?: 17, 21, 35, ___?

s.

1 february 2mil5. puerto vallarta, jalisco, mexico

steve.

We have been here in PV for three days before flying later this afternoon into the heart of Mexico for our three months in San Miguel de Allende. We've been staying with friends, so there have been a fair number of social obligations, but rest assured that all my spare time has been spent puzzling the next number in the series that begins: 17, 21, 35, __.

Your hint that it has to do with obituaries has been useless to me. Okay then, let me give you my answers. Yes, I have *two* possible answers. Now right away you know that if someone has *two* possible answers to a question like this, the chances are both are wrong. I am fully aware of this, but I feel I must toss out my answers and the thinking behind them just to show you I worked at it.

First possible answer: 49.

I get this by starting with 17 and add 4 to get 21. Now add 14 to get 35. So the next thing to add would be 24, which would give me the fourth number in the sequence as 49. Among the many problems with this answer is: what would be the significance of starting with 17? And why add 4 in the first place; where did 4 come from? And, of course, what does any of this have to do with obituaries, as per your hint?

Second possible answer: 49.

Yes, again. But this time with a different rationale. If you think of the number 17 as representing 1 x 7 (as in: xy where $x=1$ and $y=7$), then 21 represents 3 x 7, and 35 represents 5 x 7, and the next number in the sequence would be 49 or 7 x 7. So what's wrong with that? A lot. In the first place, why represent the first number in the sequence in a different way that the others? To be consistent, the sequences would have to go either 17, 37, 57, ___ ; or 7, 21, 35, ___. And, of course, again, what does any of this have to do with obituaries?

Anyway, I'm giving up. Tell me the next number. And why.

t.

3 Feb. 2005 Gilbert Arizona

Terry.

I deeply admire what you are doing with your writing, so many days in a row of at least one hour logged ….(how many days is it now?)….. I remember when you and Miranda and Kathy and I had dinner in Santa Monica you retold how one night after a California party you had to really scramble to get your one hour in under the midnight deadline to keep your streak alive. You are the Joe DiMaggio of writers now.

Here's what I admire most about your streak . . . I have always had friends who were "writers" who did everything but write. They read books like crazy, as if that were really something. And, of course reading books is a fine thing, but if one is a writer, reading books can be a dodge. Einstein once said that after a certain age it's time to stop reading and start writing, stop reading the works of others and start doing your own work.

And so I've always admired the disciplines and order in your life that led you to be a smash success financially in the creative world of advertising. It's led you to remain slim and healthy (as we chronicled your mathematical weight disciplines in *Two Guys Read Moby-Dick*). In fact your weight disciplines helped me a great deal.....I've had people call me about my picture on the cover of my new book (which I'm sending to you as soon as you give me an address in Mexico...where the hell are you, anyway? Do even *you* know? And are there any people *left* down there? It seems everybody in Mexico has crossed the border and come here! Which is good for the sport of baseball....but I digress.)

And I've often written in my previous motivational books that 1) don't envy, emulate and 2) it's never too late. That might even be a good poem:

> Don't envy,
> emulate.
> And it's never
> too late.

Because it *is* never too late. Grandma Moses was 71 when she started her career as a painter and she painted for 30 years!!!!!! A thirty-year career is no small thing! And she could paint. Kathy says I lose the impact of that example because she wasn't such a great painter, but I disagree! Moses could paint. You would like a Moses in your den and so would I. A friend would come see you and ask, "Who did that?" and you would say, "Moses."

So I decided after Santa Monica to emulate you. It helped that I'd also read Steven Pressfield's shocking slap-in-the-face to all "writers" book, *The War of Art*. What a wake-up call that book was. How that book called me out behind the bar to put up or shut up. Then, as a final shove, I read Lawrence Block's *Telling Lies For Fun and Profit*. His book about writing. His main point was that the whole thing is in the routine. One writes or doesn't. You are not a writer if you do not write.

So even though I now have seven books out there, I have been so erratic it's been pathetic. I've scrambled to meet publishers' deadlines writing long hours, then I've quit altogether for months, once I quit for a year! So I've never been a writer. Not a real one. Until now. I have my own daily discipline, modeled after yours. Daily. Even on Sunday. Even though I have a full-time speaking and coinsulting career going on, this daily work I will not abandon. Not until you read my obituary.

∾————∾

And speaking of my obituary, I will now spare you the math riddle I asked you of what number follows in this sequence: 17, 21, 35, ___. Because you have the kind of brain that receives a challenge like this one and really takes it on. I do not! Wish I did. Someone throws me such a problem and I answer it in a few smartass seconds! And then never think another thought about it. That's why there are so many people in the world today who think I'm stupid. They're wrong, as we both know, but still. They're out there. And I put them there by my own behavior. The IRS, for example, thinks I'm really stupid, but I won't go down that road right now.

Here's the problem: 17, 21, 35 is a sequence that shows up in a song on the new (and last) Ray Charles album. He sings the old classic, *It Was A Very Good Year*, a song I first heard on a Kingston

Trio album in the late 1950s that you yourself introduced me to, and a song most people remember by Frank Sinatra. The song recounts the four stages in a man's life. It starts, "When I was seventeen, it was a very good year," and then describes the conditions. It goes to the second stage, "When I was twenty-one," and the third stage, "When I was thirty-five....." and finally goes to the final stage:

> But now the days grow short
> I'm in the autumn of the year
> And now I think of my life as vintage wine
> from fine old kegs
> from the brim to the dregs
> And it poured sweet and clear
> It was a very good year
> It was a very good year

So my question to you is this: 17, 21, 35 and ??. What exactly is the autumn of one's life? To me, the jump from 35 to autumn is somewhat alarming. Shouldn't there be some more stages in there? Like, 17, 21, 35, 40, 50, 65, 80 and then winter? The song was written in the early fifties, when people thought 60 was senile and long gone. Now as we read the obits we see people dying at 98 and 93 every day. Modern medicine is the life-extender? I think it has more to do with not smoking and not eating hamburger and Wonder Bread for three meals a day. Whatever is extending life, it makes that song ridiculous and morbid to me. Grandma Moses would not have liked that song. Grandma Moses would have preferred Jan and Dean. *The Little Old Lady from Pasadena.*

Steve.

4 febrero 2005 – San Miguel de Allende, Guanajuato, MX

Steve.

The 17, 21, 35, ? riddle was great and I am kicking myself that I didn't get it because I know the song well and have always liked it. And yes, it *is* all about obituaries, in fact the song can be thought of as a personal, romantic, musical obituary.

Now while you say the last number in the sequence is up for grabs and, in fact, is affected by actuarial tables, I maintain it is quite specific (if variable). I think that last number has to be the age of the person that is singing the song at the time. So when you listen to Ray Charles singing it on his final album, the last number is 74 (or at least I think that was Ray's age when he recorded the song). When you sing the song after reading this, the final number in the sequence will be 60, because – like it or not – that's how old you are.

By the way, the version of the song I most remember was in a "duets" album and I know Willie Nelson was one of the singers, but I can't remember if the other singer was Julio Iglesias or Frank Sinatra. Yes, I know that seems like a strange thing to forget.

———

But while one mystery gets solved, another is created. In your last letter you referred to your career as "coinsulting." Now I have too much respect for you to suspect that this was a garden-variety typo. Perhaps a Freudian typo. But what I do suspect is that you're making a passing punning personal pronouncement on the nature of the consulting business.

Are you suggesting that it's lucrative? That it provides you with "coin?"

Perhaps you meant to insert a hyphen and you wanted to make the point that in this field both consultant and client insult each other's intelligence. That it's really a business of "co-insulting?"

Perhaps you intended both meanings.

At any rate I think it's an excellent neologism, though it does take away from the word's original meaning stemming from the root word "con." As in hoodwink.

———

We are now here in San Miguel after our ten days on the coast in Sayulita and Puerto Vallarta. I have scouted the available newspapers in town and find there are only two in English. First is the *Miami Herald*'s Latin American edition. Discouragingly, this paper seems to carry no obituaries. (What kind of a newspaper is this?!?) Perhaps it is only these first two days that I have been reading it, but still …

The other paper is the weekly called *Atencion*. Despite its Spanish name (there is an accent mark, which I can't manage on this computer, over the O), it is produced by the American library down here almost entirely for the English-speaking community in San Miguel. And while most of this community seems only days away from becoming obituaries themselves, the paper carries no obituaries, at least there were none in the only issue of the paper I have seen so far. A bit later today a new issue hits the streets and I have my fingers crossed for an obit or two. I'll let you know next e-mail.

In the midst of this obit-less land I went to the internet café today and tapped in the *NYTimes* on-line. Max Schmeling – 99 years old. Former German world heavyweight boxing champion. In fact, as the obit pointed out, the *only* German heavyweight champion. Did you read it? Very interesting, I thought.

When he won the championship, he was lionized by the Nazi Party. Yet he refused to join the party, refused to divorce his Czech wife (who the Nazis weren't wild about) and refused to fire his Jewish-American promoter. The Nazis would probably rather have had a little more gung-ho party man as champion, I guess. And when he lost to Joe Louis, the government totally ignored him the rest of the time they were in power.

Of course, Schmeling will forever be linked with Joe Louis because of his two fights with him. But while the world built up his second fight with Louis as the battle of Democracy vs. Nazism or Black Man vs. Aryan, Schmeling saw it pretty much as just a boxing match. I personally remember the fight clearly. Now you may, with some justice, suggest that it's impossible for me to remember a fight that took place six years before I was born. But you are forgetting the influence and staying power of our early audio memories.

At some point in the mid-1950s, my father bought an LP record of the greatest moments in sports. I must have played it quite a bit because there are a number of indelible marks left on my brain from it: Bobby Thompson's home run; Lou Gehrig's farewell speech; a Rockne pre-game locker room speech; and ... the second Louis-Schmeling fight. Louis knocked him down four times in the first round and it was officially a knockout at 2:04 of that round.

Fast forward to after the War. Schmeling is in his forties, broke and is no longer the fighter he was. But he fights another four or five fights with indifferent success because he needs the money. But instead of just blowing it, Max uses his final fight earnings to buy the exclusive German rights to sell Coca-Cola. Obviously over the next few decades Schmeling becomes a rich man.

If you recall Joe Louis's arc after he left the ring, it went the other way financially. I remember him at one point being millions in debt to the IRS. During this time, the obit said, Schmeling kept in touch with him and gave him quite a bit of money over time, when Louis was in need. And when Louis died, it was Schmeling that paid for the funeral.

What a great story, one that flies in the face of most American prejudices against Germans – especially since it involves a man who was painted to represent Germany's worldwide supremacy. That's what I love about the obits – it's that final summing up. (I believe Somerset Maugham's autobiography was called *The Summing Up*.)

Let me just hitchhike on Schmeling's death to tell you a tale that is a tiny little piece in the grand mosaic of the human comedy. It is comedy, don't you think?

I was out in Los Angeles on a television commercial shoot. It was one of the first times I had been there; I was very young, maybe 24 or so, and I was staying at a residence motel in West Hollywood called the Regency that had been recommended by someone who had stayed there before. It was quite nice really; it was like a little apartment with a kitchen and a living room as well as the bedroom. Perfect really for those times you were out in LA for a while shooting or editing and didn't want to have to go out for every breakfast, say. You could just buy some coffee and juice and maybe a loaf of bread and make yourself a light breakfast without having to leave the apartment.

What the place didn't have was a bar or restaurant or a newsstand or room service or any of the amenities a regular hotel would have. So after the first day's work I got back to the Regency and didn't feel like going out for dinner, but really didn't have much choice. I decided I'd walk down to Sunset, just a couple of blocks away, and find a place I could grab a bite. Unfortunately that stretch of Sunset didn't really have any downscale restaurants so I wound up looking at a place that seemed a bit fancier than I had really wanted. The name of the place was The Saratoga, and on the bright-lights sign in the front, underneath the restaurant name it said, "Where the show and sports people congregate."

My kind of place, I thought. I mean I'm a sports person, and I'd certainly never turn up my nose at rubbing shoulders with a few show people. I went in and was greeted by the owner, a heavy-set guy about 45 or 50 who had taken a few too many Toots Shorr lessons. He picked up right away that I wasn't a show person and I guess he'd never seen any of my better games at second base with the Wildcats in the Birmingham Babe Ruth League, so he didn't go overboard on the welcome, but still he was pleasant enough. He was going to take me to a table in the dining room, but I said if it was okay, I'd rather just sit in the bar if I could get food there. Sure, he said, and he gave me a seat on the red leather banquette that faced the bar. Great.

I remember I ordered trout amandine. It was the first time I'd ever had it and I thought it was great. I probably don't even have to mention how grown-up and worldly I felt having this dish I'd only heard of before in a restaurant which was undoubtedly swarming with show and sports people. I had a very nice hour and a half there and then paid my bill and went back to the Regency for the night. In all truth, however, I have to admit I did not personally have any show or sports people sightings.

The next evening I got finished working late and didn't get back to the Regency until about 8 o'clock. Oh well, I thought, I'll just head on down to the Saratoga again. The Toots Shorr imitator remembered me from the night before and with appropriate flourishes showed me to "my table," which was again the spot on the banquette I had warmed the night before. I ordered my trout amandine again and felt pretty sophisticated again as I had a beer, ate and watched the comings and goings at the bar. When I was having my dessert a black couple in their fifties – him in a sport coat, her in a nice simple dress – came into the bar with a white guy about the same age. I have no idea who the woman or the white guy were, but the black man was Joe Louis. I recognized him immediately.

I nursed my dessert and coffee and watched the three of them at the bar. I was thinking how much I was going to love telling my father this story. Throughout his life he never veered from the certain belief that Joe Louis was the greatest fighter that ever lived. When I finally finished and was leaving, I walked over to the bar and said to Louis, "I'm sorry to interrupt, Mr. Louis, but my father would never forgive me if I didn't shake your hand." As a bit of a non sequitur I added, "I'm from Detroit." The Joe Louis Arena was another two and a half decades from being built, but no one from Detroit needed a building to know that Joe Louis was from the city.

Louis was very welcoming and friendly. He introduced me to the others in the party and asked about my father and Detroit, questions to which I'm certain I gave strikingly insightful answers. And after maybe two or three minutes I made my excuses to leave. I apologized for interrupting their conversation, thanked them for letting me, and started for the door.

The owner, who had been standing by the door, had watched the scene and when I got to the door he pulled me aside and asked me who the guy at the bar was! Incredulously I told him, all the while thinking that here this guy runs a watering hole (as I'm sure he probably thought of it) "where the show and sports people congregate" *and he doesn't recognize Joe Louis*! Perhaps show people were his strong suit.

The other funny thing was that when I was leaving the restaurant I saw Toots making a beeline not, as I would have suspected, for the bar to introduce himself to Louis, but rather for the dining room to tell the other patrons that a sports person was congregating in the bar.

The coda to this story is that a couple of years ago Miranda and I were staying at Eunice's *[my wife's sister. TNH]* apartment in West Hollywood and I figured out that I was only a few blocks from where the Saratoga was. I made a point of working out where it would have been. The building that's there now houses a Baja

Fresh and a Coffee Bean, neither establishment offering trout amandine.

So the Saratoga is gone. Joe Louis is gone. My father is gone. Even Trout Amandine is gone. (When was the last time you saw that item on a restaurant menu? About the same time you last saw Baked Alaska?) And yet, I endure!

t.

February 7th – Gilbert, AZ

Terry.

R.I.P. Ossie Davis (no relation to Ossie Virgil or Ozzie Nelson).

Steve.

12 feb 2mil5 – San Miguel de Allende

steve

Aristotle was of the opinion that happiness was the ultimate end of life. That all the other things we desperately desire and strive for – love, money, hot women – all these other things are merely means of creating happiness. (Don't you think this tones up our correspondence, starting off with Aristotle like this? Or do you think I blew the tone with the mention of hot women?)

Anyway, I really hate to disagree with Aristotle because the guy's got a suitcase full of credentials, but I can't buy this. It all seems too simple to me, sort of the Bobby McFerrin school of life – Don't worry; be happy! Now perhaps I feel this way because I find myself, without any effort to speak of, happy pretty much all the time. I have had spells of misery, but I certainly don't intend to make a habit of it, despite the beneficial effect misery is said to have on one's writing.

So I guess I'm lucky. But at the same time, it seems to me that happy is something you either are or you aren't. I simply can't countenance the possibility that the entire goal of life is either handed to you or it isn't. Now don't get me wrong, I'm not saying I have any certain knowledge of the meaning of life, but I *do* think it has to be something you *work* for, rather than a wheel-of-fortune spin. It must be something you achieve, something you try to accomplish during your life.

I have a friend whose goal in life was to have a two-inch obituary in the *New York Times*. Now that, it seems to me, is more like it. Something you work for. He died, by the way, a few years ago at an age that had a 5 as its first number. The *New York Times* failed to note his passing. Which is odd since I believe he was a much more valid philosopher than Aristotle.

———

The curtain went down on Arthur Miller, I see, at 89. The *Miami Herald* (Mexican Edition) does not carry many obits, as I've noted before, but they did carry his. Front page even.

The *New York Times* version of Miller's life (which I read on-line) was pretty much: He wrote an important play when he was 33, and at 43 he married Marilyn Monroe. Period. They didn't really think much of the last 46 years of his life. Still, his obituary was measured in column-feet instead of column-inches, so by my friend's standard, he did good.

———

Do you remember going with me to see Arthur Miller speak in New York at a YMCA on the Upper West Side? Kay was with us and so was Miranda. It must have been around 1990 or so. There were two or three other speakers first and, like most literary events, it was running a little late.

Finally Arthur Miller came on. We listened to him for maybe fifteen minutes and then, because we had reservations at Café des Artistes, we walked out of the auditorium. Kay laughed about that later and said that she told all her friends in Richmond about how we "walked out on Arthur Miller." Well, now he's walked out on us.

Of course, I have a soft spot for him because – next to Tom Brady – he's probably the most important play-maker the University of Michigan has ever produced.

t.

ps. I'm surprised you weren't on Arthur Miller before me.

2/13/05 – Gilbert AZ

Terry,

I would have been on Miller, but I couldn't remember who he was … he wrote "Bees" or something? (Actually he was reading his short story about bees when we walked out on him.) He was like Tom Tresh and Clint Hurdle, right? Looked like a world-beater in his youth but just mediocre from then on. Preachy, wasn't he? Too much message and not enough style or humor or brains, that Arthur Miller? Confused, romantically? Married Diana Dors?

s.

14 February 2005 – Valentine's Day – SMA

steve.

Have you heard of the book *Sophie's World*? I'm reading it right now because, although it's a novel, the book is supposed to give you a cocktail-conversation-level mastery of the history of philosophy and I figure that should be plenty good enough for my needs.

Anyway, early on in the book, the title character, Sophie, thinks: "You can't experience being alive without realizing that you have to die. But it's just as impossible to realize you have to die without thinking how incredibly amazing it is to be alive."

Some people apparently find our correspondence a bit ghoulish. Frankly I don't – at all. In fact I'm always surprised when, after I explain our project, I get in return an odd look. I have found Sophie's realization to be true. Dealing in obituaries and thinking about death as much as I have since we started this, I have been quite overwhelmed by and alert to the wonders of being alive. Seriously.

I would bet you a comprehensive research study would reveal morticians to be the occupational group most charged with the joy of life. You think?

⌒══════⌒

By the way, speaking of comprehensive research studies, I read some good news for us the other day. In a story on something else, it was mentioned *en passant* in the *Miami Herald* that it has long been known that people with high IQs tend to live longer than the dimwits we're forced to share the earth with. Study after study has shown this apparently, though there is some question as to whether this is due to the fact that the higher IQ people tend to go into lower-risk occupations. (Who cares?)

⌒══════⌒

And finally – and then I'll get out of your hair – there was a lecture down here the other day about what happens to you after you die. I know you'll think I let down the side, but Miranda and I went to a movie (*De-Lovely*) instead.

I considered going to the after-death talk, but I carefully reviewed the speaker's bio and it seemed to me that she lacked the one credential that would have given her speech some real authority. It seems that she is still alive.

Ah, Steve, this place is swarming with amiable macadamia nuts.

t.

15 February 2005 Gilbert

Terry,

I absolutely hated Arthur Miller's pretentious ponderous writing almost as much as I hated his bitter sophomoric misunderstanding of the free enterprise system and its sales process which is why I had to write the definitive counter to *Death of a Salesman* when I wrote *The Joy of Selling*, hailed by most critics as the last word on the subject so clumsily opened by Miller. (I noted today that *The Joy of Selling* is ranked #234,511 on Amazon's sales rankings, which means that there are a couple hundred thousand books outselling it today. So maybe the public hasn't elevated it to Miller status yet, but there's time (*The Crucible* sold six million copies in paperback!)

I read a lot of Miller's short pieces that he wrote later in life, and he was just uniformly awful. One of those pieces we walked out on! Would we have walked out on Dylan Thomas? I think not.

You yourself also come from the University of Michigan and you are a better writer. He is more "important" than you are at the moment, but important to whom? If someone handed you one book by an "important" writer and another by a "wonderful" writer which one would you rather read?

I put Miller up there with that other ponderously pretentious fellow about whom you and I just finished writing an entire book, Herman Melville. (Actually, our book, *Two Guys Read Moby-Dick*, used the reading of *Moby-Dick* as a mere jumping off point so that we could dilate joyfully on many subjects. Had it just been about Melville I think we would have had trouble finishing the project.)

I had occasion to mention that book today because a friend of mine Steve Davis had just returned from Maui where "we must have seen a hundred whales!" I told him about our recent trip on the whale watching boat in Halifax, Nova Scotia, during which we saw no whales! It occurred to me that anyone could charge for "whale-watching" as long as you noted up front that there were no guarantees. I could set up a little Jeep-riding whale-watching venture here outside of Phoenix, and because it is the desert here I think I'd have the market all to myself. I'd just have to be very up front and blunt about there being no guarantees. "I'll be honest, we may not even see a whale."

s.

ps. (Your writing has taken off...your humor is your writing's poetry and spirit and exactly what other writers cannot do...try as they might)

Steve.

Thanks for your more-than-lavish praise. Again. It gets embarrassing thanking you all the time for your compliments on my writing, but to be perfectly honest, I have no difficulty living with this embarrassment. To inject a note of realism into this, however, did it ever occur to you that just possibly we like each other's humor because we have the *same* sense of humor – a wry mix of human psychology, uncommon sense and dada forged on the mean streets of the Birmingham, Michigan, of our youth? Perhaps we are only funny to each other.

On the other hand, neither one of us seems to have any trouble making other people laugh. This despite the fact that neither one of us tells "jokes." So I guess I am forced to come to the conclusion that we're just downright hilarious guys.

Terry (2.15.2005)

15 Feb. 2005 Gilbert

terry.

Karl Haas died. Not many people know who he was. He was a deejay of sorts, but he played classical music and had a studio in his home in Detroit. More than a deejay, he was an on-air professor. He was 91 last week when he died. I remember him because I used to sneak time listening to him. It wasn't cool to listen to what did not rock in those days when we lived near Detroit and were young, you and I. But I loved his show. So it was a secret of mine. He was so low key and bright and I loved the way he explained the classical music that he played. His soft, erudite explanations were better than the music, especially to me a teenager outside Detroit thrilling to Martha and the Vandellas and Jackie Wilson. Karl Haas was a secret addiction. I've always wanted to understand classical music. And had I spent enough time with Karl Haas I just might have. I'm glad he got to have 91 years. You could tell by his voice and his quiet enthusiasm that he was a happy man, doing what he loved. Who would not want to listen to that?

steve.

19 February 2005 – San Miguel

Steve.

You will recall that I have commented several times on the paucity of obituaries in the Mexican edition of the *Miami Herald* that we get down here. Perhaps you even think I am over-doing this. But I persist: I find it odd.

Well, today in the paper, comes an explanation. Or at least a possible explanation. It comes in an article on another phenomenon that I had noticed in the Spanish Mexican newspapers.

Last week, for instance, the *Reforma*, which seems to be the most prestigious of the Mexican papers, was filled with ads – some of them quite large – expressing condolences to the family of an 18-year-old girl who was killed in a boating accident. There were a lot of ads. Would you consider 147 ads a lot? That's how many there were. None of these ads said anything other than sort of a "deepest sympathy" message. Even just casually flipping through the paper you would have been prompted to ask, "Hey, what's all this about?"

A few days later came a story in the *Herald*, written by a *Washington Post* reporter who had noted these condolences ads and asked, "Hey, what's all this about?" Well, he must be a young reporter because otherwise he'd know that all curious, otherwise-unexplainable behaviors have as their root cause either love or money. The cause of this phenomenon is money. Apparently these ads are a common thing in Mexico after someone of some importance, especially in business or government, dies. The point of the ads is to show how close you are or were to the power or the influence. And you certainly don't want your competitor to show his sympathy in this public way without your ad being there too.

The father of the 18-year-old girl, it turns out, is a very prominent businessman. Some of the 147 ads were from individuals, but most were from companies that deal or *want* to deal with his company. From what the story said, no one can afford *not* to pony up for one of these expensive ads. Names are taken: scores are kept. (This is fine by the *Reforma* which estimates that 10% of their advertising revenue comes from these condolences ads!)

All of which I found interesting as another facet of the death industry. But even more interesting, I thought, were the side comments in the story about the Mexican attitude toward death.

In the first place the story pointed out – as is fairly well known because of the national celebration of the Day of the Dead here – Mexicans have a very open relationship with death. Death isn't seen as horrible, but rather as a natural consequence of life. However, it is also considered a private thing. In fact, Mexican newspapers really do not have obituaries as we would know them in the U.S. or Europe. As a rule, the newspapers here will only run obituaries of extremely well-known political leaders or celebrities. Last year, the *Reforma* experimented with what they called U.S.-style obits, but the items were hated by the Mexicans who found them in bad taste. They felt the obits treated deaths as news events instead of private family matters. *Reforma* no longer runs them.

Another oddity pointed out was that while it is proper to express condolences, asking how someone died simply isn't done.

All of this led me to believe that maybe this attitude toward obituaries is the reason the Mexican edition of the *Herald* doesn't run obituaries. Now this would make a lot of sense except for the fact that the *Herald* is published in English, so one would suspect its readers are American. And Americans, as we know (and count on to insure booming sales for this book) *love* obituaries.

Perhaps the publishers of the paper are under the impression that when Americans are in Mexico, they adopt Mexican sensibilities. If this is the case, I can assure you that based on my observation of the Americans down here, they are totally mistaken. Most of them in fact, consider the country more-or-less Southern Arizona and are affronted when the check out girl at the *supermercado* doesn't understand English.

t.

2-20-05 Gilbert

Terry,

You mentioned a couple of days ago that the word out of Miami is that people with high IQs tend to live longer than the "dimwits" they're forced to share the earth with ... interesting in light of this:

When I was doing research for a book I found a cover story in *LIFE* magazine, and it was about a convent full of nuns. Something weird was happening at the convent! The nuns there were living longer than they were supposed to, much longer. The average age of death for women was in the mid-seventies, but the nuns at the convent were living an average of 20 years longer than that. Some were in their hundreds!

The convent housed the Sisters of Notre Dame in Mankato, Minnesota, and brain researchers from UCLA believed the nuns had discovered a major secret of long life: the exercise of the human brain. The mother superior in the convent long believed that "an idle mind is the devil's workshop" and so her sisters did not let their minds go idle.

s.

20 Feb 2005 SMA

steve.

Seems to me that the Sisters of Notre Dame story is not about active brains, but constitutes rather the long-awaited indisputable proof for the existence of God! He cares! And gives those who kowtow to him additional decades of life!!

t.

2-20-05 Gilbert

Terry,

In reference to your astute speculation on Valentine's Day about morticians' awareness and joy of life, I must say that when I was going to college I had a part time job in a hospital, and the people who worked Emergency, the doctors and nurses there, closest to trauma and death, the ones who saw the most dramatic deaths, were the life … I almost said the life of the party! Because they were always the most ALIVE people there. They had high energy, good cheer and humor. Most people would imagine that they would be the most depressed. But no.

Maybe death gives us life. So many stories like the one about the person who finds out she has only six months to live, and so she makes every second count and lives in a newer fuller way than ever before! Precious life! Look at Anthony Burgess! An unfocused lazy intellect and writer until, no, UNTIL! he learned that he had a fatal disease and only a few months, MONTHS! to live, so he got into hyper-space action writing furiously, night and day, novel after novel so his wife and kid would have royalties when he was gone … and lo … and lo and behold, he survived! Misdiagnosis! He lived! And went on to write over 50 books including *Clockwork Orange* …

What gave him that new life? Death gave him life! Our high school troubadour Hap Dunne once wrote a song or was in the process of writing a song called *Dead Leaves in Our Pockets* or some such title about dead leaves and for a tree to shed leaves, exfoliate them, is like all the stuff in us humans that dies every second, skin cells, all kinds of cells dying, dying, dying, and shuffling off to Buffalo this mortal coil, and all this death death death gives us new life.

s.

2-21-05 gilbert-az

dear t

One of my true heroes committed suicide yesterday and I will probably have more to say about him and his weird life and rude death, but for now I had to satisfy something restless in my mind … a thought I had posed before in this correspondence … a riddle: If someone can still make you laugh, can they be dead? Maybe their body is useless now, but their mind might still connect.

So I took down my old worn copy of Dr. Hunter Thompson's *Great Shark Hunt* and turned to his story, "The Kentucky Derby is Decadent and Depraved," because it was always my favorite piece of his writing. And despite being tired and ready for a nap, I found myself laughing again, against my will, at the deep hilarity of the writing.

Most "funny" writers are light, using surface humor and wiseacre gags to sweeten their writing. But not the doctor. (He was a doctor of journalism.) Dr. Thompson had a deep and disturbing humor that lined up your soul and gave it a warm direct shot. His writing makes you laugh when you read it, and laugh again when you think back on it. And because the humor is so deep, there is no punch line to grow old in it. Every twisted and violently amusing word picture punches afresh. In the stomach.

He's a true hero of mine for that. For being able to do that with words. Even after he is dead.

s.

21 feb 2005 – SMA

Steve.

Hadn't seen *any* newspaper in three days, so I checked out the *Times* on-line today and discovered that Hunter Thompson had joined the Do-It-Yourself Club. I thought of you immediately, knowing your love of his writing.

It was clearly a breaking story when I read it, so they just had the basic facts ("self inflicted gunshot wound" in his own home) without any of the whys. Did he have some disease? Suffer from bouts of depression? What? Still, was it really a surprise? I think he would have ranked in the top 5 on anybody's most-likely-to-commit-suicide list, don't you?

I spent much of the day trying to wrap my mind around what I thought of him.

It strikes me that he could symbolize the rather different directions *our* lives took in our mid-twenties. I remember you early on as a very big Hunter Thompson enthusiast. And despite your basic political positions being at times very different from his, over the years you have always been a fan.

I suspect that as much as the writing, it was the "gonzo" life that writing represented that was a major part of the attraction. It was very much a lifestyle that you, along with a lot of others our age, were drawn to. For my part, I might have had romantic dreams of that kind of lifestyle, but I was really not going to let myself get that much out of control. It's easy to suggest that this difference between us at the time was due to the fact that I was married and had a child by the time I was 21. Certainly that was a part of it, but much more determining, I think, is a basic caution and timidity built into my make-up. You are, or were then anyway, much more headlong. You may say some of that personality was due to the drinking and the drugs, but I strongly suspect it was the other way around – that the drinking and the drugs were a result of a natural inclination to the gonzo.

Anyway, all of these thoughts came up primarily because, although I've always held a general regard for Thompson, I have never read one of his books. I have read a few of his magazine pieces (and now really want to read the Derby piece) and was always sort of appalled by the chaos – not the chaos of the writing, but rather the chaos of his life. No matter how much living that way might liberate my writing, I am constitutionally unable to consider it.

Of course now you live a much more sane life. Do you think it affects your writing?

And then later in the day Miranda brings home the *Miami Herald* with the news that Sandra Dee is D. Somehow the *NYTimes* missed it, but she also died on Sunday. Could it be that the news of Gidget's death was what caused Hunter to pull the trigger?

t.

21-feb PHX-AZ

terry.

I hear you on the lifestyle of Hunter. I tried to match it! But the lifestyle was not as important to me as the writing was. Hunter Thompson could really, really write, and I didn't care what his politics or drug use was or wasn't, he could really write … one of the five best writers alive in my lifetime. The Kentucky Derby story which Tom Wolfe cited in a tribute piece (after he must have somehow found out that I had cited it) could not even have been written by Wolfe … and *Fear and Loathing in Las Vegas* is one of the ten most beautifully and powerfully written books of all time. It was the writing. Even his ESPN columns at the end were great writing. He once re-typed all of Hemingway's books … now, in heaven, Hemingway is re-typing all of the good doctor's books. He was a hero of mine.

s.

23-feb

steve.

We had dinner last night at a local bullfighting hangout (I know that sounds odd and unlikely, but I don't know what else to call it. The name is Ole-Ole.) here with a photographer Miranda had met in Spanish conversation sessions at the San Miguel Library. He used to be the publisher/editor of a weekly newspaper in North Carolina, which he sold sometime back. An interesting guy with a rich southern accent and a colorful way of talking. Interestingly he was a grandson of Sherwood Anderson. (His girlfriend was amazed that we had heard of Anderson. Obviously she hadn't when she met him.)

Anyway, I mention this, and his newspaper background, because when we were settled in at our table and the drinks had arrived, this guy raised his glass and said: "Well, let's drink this one to Hunter Thompson." He was also obviously a fan.

All of which is making me determined to read something of his. (You recommend *F&LiLV*? Or should I start with a collection of his essays? I'd like to read that Derby piece.)

Terry.

25 Feb. 2005 PHX az

Terry,

You write to say that in a cantina in Mexico someone has raised a glass to toast the memory of Hunter Thompson. I am spending the weekend re-reading my favorite pieces by him, and there are many, this could last a year. He is one of the five best writers of our age, in my opinion.

Thompson is always referencing lines from songs by Dylan, John Prine and Warren Zevon, and I recall he once wrote in Rolling Stone, "The music business is a cruel and shallow money trench, a long plastic hallway where thieves and pimps run free, and good men die like dogs. There's also a negative side."

Wow, music and death, a good combination if you are living in Mexico, as you are. Because "Deguello," which loosely translated means "slit throat," was what Santa Ana's band played nightly outside the Alamo, followed by a cannon barrage. Essentially the message was no quarter would be taken, and all would die. (In the movie *Alamo*, David Crockett accompanies it one night – hence the soundtrack song name "Deguello de Crockett" – for 60 seconds of battle-stopping music.)

In *Rio Bravo*, the movie you sent to me and Kathy, starring Ricky Nelson, John Wayne and Dean Martin, that "Deguello" tune is played by the band in the saloon to foretell ominous death, and in one scene Walter Brennan's character plays along with it on his harmonica in the sheriff's office, in defiance of the threat.

If you hear that song at night outside your apartment played more than once, GET OUT OF MEXICO! Or, short of that, pick up a guitar and play with it, as Crockett and Brennan did. Chords: Am, C, F, G, Am.

s.

26 feb. – San Miguel de Allende

steve.

I will do as you say if I hear the tune. But I must say the name Deguello does not, in the absence of context, sound very threatening to me. It sounds more like the name of a hot new prospect for the Tigers – a slick-fielding shortstop: Luis Deguello.

t.

27 Feb. 2005 PHX az

Terry,

As I receive these postcards and letters from you from Mexico, I often glance up at a photo of you on our kitchen wall, from Mexico, from many years ago, when we were down in Mazatlan, drinking beer, and acting wild as always ... fighting waves as they came in ... you and I and Fred going into the water and actually trying to battle the waves and turn them back out to sea. (Hunter Thompson would get this immediately ... the importance of being a drunken wave-fighter.)

Then comes this missive today from while you were in Sayulita ... hand-written and not designed for this book but for my eyes and Kathy's (to whom I have not sufficiently explained the importance of wave-fighting) ... I laugh as I read it, and drop it down to the coffee table, then later hear her laughing while reading it, so I insist that I put it here, because it is about death ... about death's opposite, Dylan Thomas's request that we not go gently, that we rage against the dying of the light:

> "Steve,
>
> Do not think I did not hear the whispers.
> He is sixty, they said; he has lost the
> alertness, perhaps the courage too. The
> waves look bigger when one gets older.
> And these last three years he has only
> fought in fresh water, which is not
> the same is it?
>
> And yet, as I stepped on the beach
> in Sayulita to once again fight Pacific
> Waves, I saw my duty clearly and
> felt the strength within me rise.
> The waves are relentless, but so too
> the wave fighter. I did my job. How

well? That is for others to judge. But
let me just say that had I been in
Indonesia at Christmas, I believe
hundreds, if not thousands, of lives
would have been saved.

Yours in the brotherhood,
Terrence N. "Terry" Hill
WFI – Wave Fighters International
33 years service – and counting.

27 Feb 2005 – SMA, MX

Steve,

In the *NYT* obits today, two "Patts" with connections to our
youth – or mine anyway. Edward Patten and Tom Patterson.

Edward Patten was a Pip. For 24 years, along with various of
his cousins, he backed Gladys Knight. You can hear him on "I
Heard It Through the Grapevine" at the beginning of *The Big Chill*,
in my opinion, the best University of Michigan film ever made,
easily beating out the distant second *Harmon of Michigan*.

(Okay, so tell me what the two top University of Arizona films
are?)

It is a pretty standard assumption that growing up around
Detroit in the sixties we must have been well steeped in Motown
music. Later in life when people I had just met found out I was from
Detroit, the discovery would invariably be followed up by some
Motown trivia question like, "Who played drums on 'Baby Love?'"
How should I know?

I don't know about you, but I was barely aware of Motown
music at the time. I remember liking Frankie Lymon and the
Teenagers, but I'll bet you they weren't actually Motown performers
though their sound was very like it. Why weren't we onto Motown
at the start? (Or is my memory of your musical tastes faulty?) It
seems strange to me. After all we were both deeply interested in
music, how'd we miss the hometown favorite sons and daughters.

It wasn't until much later that I got to like the Motown stuff –
like 20 years later. And even then there are huge gaps in what I like.
For instance, I can't name you a single Marvin Gaye song (and
Miranda is a *big* fan), likewise Stevie Wonder.

Moving north now, Tom Patterson was the founder of the
Stratford Shakespeare Festival in Stratford, Ontario. When I was
living in Toronto I was the writer for a documentary television
series that told the stories of various people who had taken big risks
in their lives. One of the stories I did was Tom Patterson. It really
is a remarkable story, you should use it in one of your books.

Tom was just a 30-year-old reporter for the Stratford paper and
on no other basis than that the name of the town was Stratford and
it had a river called the Avon running through it, he decided the
town should be the home of a Shakespeare Festival. He heard that
Tyrone Guthrie was in New York, talked the town council into
buying him a ticket down there and then just knocked on the
director's hotel room door. From that inauspicious beginning he
somehow made the whole thing come together. He had a dream; he
chased it; he caught it.

I've been to the Stratford Festival probably a dozen times in my
life. Miranda and I almost went last year in fact, but at the last
minute couldn't go. But the first time ever was in the summer of
1964. I had been seeing Trudi for several years, and we were both
home for summer vacation from college at the time. She had come
up with the idea of us going away to Stratford together for a
weekend.

To remind you how things have changed, Trudi's mother made
the "hotel" arrangements, which consisted of Trudi's staying at the
YWCA, which had a midnight curfew, and me staying at the
YMCA. Her mother had called and personally spoken to the Y
administrator. Still the whole thing was very exciting for us because
we were 18 and 20 and feeling very adult going off like this for the
weekend.

You and I were working at Mackworth Rees that summer and the plan was for Trudi to pick me up at the factory at 3:30 when we got off work in her father's car. Almost as embarrassing as having grown up around Detroit and not knowing anything about Motown music, is having grown up around Detroit and not knowing anything about cars. Which gets to the point that I can't remember the make of the car Trudi's father owned. It was some foreign made sports car with a convertible top.

We worked on the second floor of the factory and I remember looking down and seeing Trudi waiting there a few minutes before we were due to get off. Word of my plans had gotten around so guys – and women – were looking out and commenting on the car, on Trudi, etc. When we got off, I washed up and then went down to the car, hopped in and, with waves to you and the others, took off for a weekend in Canada.

We had a great time I remember, but I also remember with a personal pain – only slightly allayed by the knowledge that I was 20 years old at the time – that it was a big thing for me to want to impress those co-workers in the factory with Trudi (who was certainly pretty as they come) *[and who would later become my first wife. TNH]*, with the flashy sports car, with a whole golden-boy-American-prince image of myself. Even now it makes me blush to think about it.

I'm having a lot of these feelings of mortification and embarrassment lately since I've been spending a bit of time putting together thoughts and notes in order to write a longish piece on the Deke House at Michigan during the time I was there (1962-66). Time and again in recalling incidents from those years I am stunned to realize what a total, puffed-up snob I was then. And *what* did I have to be a snob about? (Interestingly, but perhaps not surprisingly, it is Trudi who comes off the best of all the people I recall in these recollections.)

Perhaps I am still a snob – I suspect we all are about some things – but it seems to me that I am a snob about much more valid things now. (But I note I still marry beautifully.) Then again, perhaps not; perhaps if I live another forty years I will look back at what I am now and flinch.

Still, I find this whole examination of myself at 20 rather disheartening. Who said the unexamined life is not worth living? I think I could have lived very well without re-picturing the Terry Hill of 1964.

t.

28 Feb.2005
Gilbert, Arizona

Terry,

You asked about the two top University of Arizona films, and I believe they were *Animal House* starring John Belushi and *Girl Happy* starring Elvis Presley.

Steve

5 march 2005 – SMA

Steve.

Do you remember Carl Tasseff? I am surprised that I recall him so well. Died in Florida last week at 76. (The same issue of the *Herald* that tells me of Carl's death also informs me that the average life expectancy is now up to 77.6 years. So I guess Carl didn't quite make it.)

The way Tasseff sticks out in my mind reminds me of the importance of football cards (and baseball cards, of course) in our lives when we were kids. Because that's the way I remember him – his football card. He played in the NFL for 12 years, but the card I distinctly remember was from the year we met in sixth grade. I doubt I ever saw him play. Or if I did I didn't much notice him. But his card!

It seems doubtful that Taseff was given a rare *Herald* obit just because of his 1954 football card. Do you think it could have been because he was Don Shula's roommate in college at John Carroll University? Remember, this is a Miami paper.

For the record, I also remember from that year – just to name a few – the cards of Rick Casares, Billy Vessels and (Something: Fred?) Cone, a fullback for the Green Bay Packers, who were horrible in those years. With the possible exception of Casares, I don't believe any of those players were candidates for anybody's All-Star team, but I remember their cards clearly. Do kids collect cards anymore or do they just play video games? Do I sound like an old man?

t.

6 March 2005 gilbert AZ

terry,

I found out today that Viva McGary McComb has died. She was 110. Born in Houston on March 29, 1894, McComb died Thursday, just days before the Conroe Pan American Round Table, which she founded in 1949, planned to recognize her as the oldest living Texan at its state convention in El Paso this weekend. McComb's life spanned 20 U.S. presidents.

I hope I live to be 110 because I have always wanted to see my 19 year old son turn 70. It would be a shame not to be there. Wonder what they'll be serving? Oh well, I'll just have to wait and see!!!

s.

7 March 2005 – San Miguel de Allende

steve,

Do you think there might be a clue to Viva McGary McComb's longevity in her first name?

I, like you, am now working on my 12th President. Unlike you, I cannot deny that last October I was certainly hoping I'd be working on number 13 by now.

Oh, did I tell you I've officially changed my name?

Sincerely,
Terrence Centenarian Hill

mar 9, 2005 gilbert az

ter,

Death visits prior to death. Does it not? Don't we "die" when we go into a deep Delta brain wave dreamless sleep? Do Samurai not learn to die before going into battle? And meditators experience a form of death, too, in their deepest states, as EKG machines verify. And Phil and Don die each time they hear the sound: "Here he comes; that's Cathy's clown."

A week or so ago Martin Denny died in his nineties. He was a bandleader who pioneered the "Tiki" sound, with various band members giving off birdcalls and such during such hits as "Quiet Village," which I remember from my youth.

His sound was pleasant and he lived a long and good life...but would he have wanted this to be in his obit? I don't know, but here it is: *"The pioneering British industrial-music group Throbbing Gristle dedicated its 'Greatest Hits' album to Mr. Denny."*

Should I be embarrassed to not have any Throbbing Gristle albums? Or any industrial music at all around the house? "Quiet Village" was meant to be mellow. Wasn't it? I don't know. How should I know?

s.

11 mar 2005 – SMA

steve.

I have to admit I don't remember Martin Denny, the "Tiki" sound or "Quiet Village." Where was I? One would think a band in which the members did various bird impressions would stick in one's mind. Did they do any barnyard animals?

Is the "Tiki" sound, the sound of Giants' running back Tiki Barber bursting through the line into the secondary?

t.

march 12 – gilbert-az

terry.

If I played you "Quiet Village," you'd remember it.

s.

20 march 2005 – San Miguel de Allende

steve.

I browse the *New York Times* obits on the internet every day or two. But I must say nothing lately struck me enough to make me want to write you. Still I always find them interesting; don't you?

For instance in the last few days there was the Glenn "Mr. Outside" Davis obit with the odd fact that you pointed out to me – that at the time of his death, Davis was married to the former wife of Alan "The Horse" Ameche. I must admit that if you had asked me before reading that if any woman had been married to both a Heisman Trophy winner and a Heisman Trophy runner-up, I'm pretty sure I would have said no. (The other interesting fact in that obit, which I thought rather cruel of the *NYT* to point out, was that Davis had flunked math in his freshman year at the Military Academy.)

Then there was the Dick Radatz obit, which, in merely citing some of his stats, pointed up how dramatically the role of the relief pitcher has changed in baseball within our lifetimes. In 1964, Radatz not only led the league in saves, he was also 16-9 in 79 relief appearances and 157 innings. Imagine any closer today pitching 157 innings OR having 25 decisions! And I think of Radatz as being in the "modern era" of relief pitchers.

Walter Cronkite's wife died. You know, I certainly remember Cronkite as a news anchor, but my more vivid memory of him is as the host of a television show called *You Are There*. Do you remember it?

And Joe Carter, 78, member of the famous Carter Family. Pallbearers included Tom T. Hall and John Carter Cash.

But despite all of these little nuggets from the *Times* notices, the one that finally prompted me to write was from the *Miami Herald*. As I've written, that paper isn't big on obits, but occasionally you'll find a few lines about a recent death in a column or a round-up section. Such was the case with Prentice Gautt. Does the name strike a chord?

It sounded awfully familiar to me, though I wouldn't have been able to identify him. He was, in 1956, the first black football player at the University of Oklahoma. Because of alumni pressure, coach Bud "The Coward" Wilkinson wouldn't give him a scholarship, but a group of black doctors and pharmacists donated money for Gautt to go to the University. Naturally he became a star. He also graduated and continued on to get a PhD in psychology.

Reading this reminded me of Bear Bryant's going out on a limb and integrating the Alabama football team. He got a lot of praise for it from civil rights people, black and white, but he said quite clearly that it was not altruism, but football that motivated him. He did it because he didn't want to see Alabama become a second rate football team. He was sick and tired of seeing some of the best high school players in the state going north to Big Ten schools because they weren't allowed to play for 'Bama.

Roll Tide!

terry.

3/21/2005 Gilbert Az

ter

Thanks for letting me know about the death of Prentice Gautt. Yes, I remember him well! Playing for Oklahoma! But didn't realize he was their first black.

Also dying this week was Bobby Short, the black cabaret/jazz singer who played for 35 years at the Carlyle hotel in New York where Kathy and I saw him on our honeymoon four years ago.

Bobby Short wrote an autobiography called *Black and White Baby*, in which he recalled living as a child among many white people "on a pleasant street, in a pleasant neighborhood where the houses had front and back yards. I am a Negro who has never lived in the South, thank God, nor was I ever trapped in an urban ghetto," he wrote. "There was a total absence of any kind of overt prejudice in those years, and it was kept that way by our teachers – which I was not aware of then. I never expected to be treated differently than my classmates."

Well, that's not exactly *Soul on Ice* or the *Autobiography of Malcolm X*. And it reminds me that the piano keys are black and white, too, or, in the words of Paul McCartney and Stevie Wonder, "ebony and ivory" living "side by side on the piano keyboard, oh lord why can't we?"

s.

22 March 2005 – San Miguel de Allende, GTO, Mexico

steve.

How appropriate that I should put down the abbreviation for the Mexican state of Guanajuato – GTO – at the head of this e-mail. Because John DeLorean, the man behind the creation of the first "muscle car," the Pontiac GTO, died on Friday. And received an 1100-word obituary in the *New York Times*.

You had probably left Detroit by the time he became a household name there, but for me he symbolized what made Detroit such a dead-end city. The problem with Detroit is that it's a company town. The fact that the "company" is actually three companies doesn't make it any the less a company town. If you work there, in one way or another you make your living off cars.

For instance, when I started in advertising in Detroit in 1966, on the surface it looked like a pretty good advertising town. There were at least ten reasonably-sized agencies; you could earn a good living at it; you got to work on very visible campaigns with big budgets. The problem was that no matter which agency you worked at, you worked on cars. And Detroit was so insular and the automotive companies and executives were so much into each other's pockets, that Detroit car advertising all looked very much the same. And since the *cars* all looked essentially the same too, you could pretty much switch the logos at the bottoms of the ads and no one would really notice.

Plus the ads were all written not to make sense to some potential buyer in Atlanta or Denver, but to some peer rival-company executive across town.

As an example, I once wrote a headline that touted the Chrysler Newport as: "The lowest priced 4-door in the mid-priced luxury field." I had actually recommended a totally different headline, saying that I didn't think one person in a hundred could tell you what the "mid-priced luxury field" was. I'll stick with that estimate to this day. The dozen or so people in the room at the time, however, all thought I was crazy. After all, *they* all knew what the "mid-priced luxury field" was. What's more, they knew that all their friends in Birmingham and Grosse Pointe and Bloomfield Hills would know what the "mid-priced luxury field" was. They were so Detroit-centric they simply couldn't conceive of anyone who didn't know which cars were in the "mid-priced luxury field." The headline was approved.

DeLorean bucked the whole system and the whole Detroit way of thinking. Of course, as with anyone perceived as an outsider, he was tolerated – and even rewarded – while he was successful, but crucified when he fell to the level of merely good. DeLorean was *very* successful at the start and he was anointed. The youngest-ever general manager of Pontiac. Four years later, the youngest-ever general manager of Chevrolet. Odds-on choice to be the youngest-ever head of General Motors.

But …

He dated movie stars.

He lived a flashy lifestyle.

He wore sideburns.

He produced fast, sexy-looking cars.

He dyed his hair for Christ's sake.

They fired him. Or that's the story at any rate.

After that he had his brief blaze of founding a company and producing a car that bore his own name. Then the collapse of the company. The bankruptcy difficulties. The investigation into his finances. The drug-bust. The legal hassles. And now, of course, the greatest indignity of all.

The thing is, DeLorean was born and raised in Detroit. He knew what the city was like. He was presumably smart. Surely he could see how it would all end if he stayed in Detroit. Why couldn't he follow our examples and get out of Detroit as soon as possible?

Well, he's out now.

Terry.

March 23, 2005

t.

I liked how you linked DeLorean to Detroit, and the collapse of both. A new documentary about Detroit will premiere this week at the University of Michigan, and it's called: *Detroit: Ruin of a City.* A kind of obituary for Detroit.

In the film French sociologist Loc Wacquant is nearly speechless as he gazes at vacant houses with sagging porches and trails of stained brick leading from the walls to the weed-choked lawns. "If it was a city of one million white people, of course you wouldn't have this urban decay, of course there would have been renewal, of course there would have been government intervention to bring in market forces that would benefit the city."

If there were enough white people in the city, according to this sociologist, there would have been the government imposition of beauty and cleanliness. Of course we know that the government has done that to Bloomfield Hills, Michigan. (And most recently Scarsdale, New York, and Beverly Hills, California.) As soon as it was determined that enough white people lived there, the government moved in with teams of cleaners and beautifiers. You can't fool the French when it comes to understanding America.

As we head toward death, we read the obituaries. Nabokov thinks about death as he begins his autobiography, *Speak Memory.* He writes, "Common sense tells us that our existence is but a brief crack of light between two eternities of darkness. Although the two are identical twins, man, as a rule, views the prenatal abyss with more calm than the one he is heading for (at some forty-five hundred heartbeats an hour.)"

Which calls to mind Alan Watts, a Zen philosopher who used to ask his seminar audiences, "Why are you so afraid of death? You've already been there. You were there before you were born, and it was just fine, wasn't it?"

To be honest? It was heaven. But it was also a little on the empty side.

s.

25 March – SMA

Steve.

Your line about the abyss we came from and presumably are going to ("It was heaven. But it was also a little on the empty side.") would be, I think, a pretty good description of growing up in Birmingham, Michigan.

t.

March 30.

terry.

I mentioned Nabokov talking about two darknesses, one prenatal and one after death. And our life now being a light between the two. The poet Robert Creeley died this week, so his light is now out. Here is a poem of his that also refers to the darkness that surrounds us:

As I sd to my

friend, because I am
always talking, – John, I
sd, which was not his
name, the darkness sur-
rounds us, what
can we do against

it, or else, shall we &
why not, buy a goddamn big car,
drive, he sd, for
christ's sake, look
out where yr going.

Steve.

31 March 2005 – SMA

steve.

I have been lately noting the lengths of various obituaries and wondering if we could measure a person's life by the number of words in his obituary. Well obviously that's a facetious proposition because we cannot leave it up to the *New York Times* or any newspaper to measure a man's worth. Surely that must be the assignment of some higher being, though the existentialists would say that that higher being is yourself.

But the raw *NYT*'s numbers are of some interest I believe.

John DeLorean, 1100 words. Bobby Short, 1700 words. Johnny Cochran, 1600 words. Robert Creeley, 260 words.

Obviously the sample is small here so one can't extrapolate to broad conclusions. You have to look at them on a case-by-case basis. For instance, someone quick on the trigger could fire off the opinion that there's a race card being played here. I mean here you have the two black men, at least arguably no more important in their fields than the two white guys were in theirs. And yet, the majority of the ink is black. One by one, though:

Bobby Short gets the longest obit, not because he was black, but because this is the *New York Times* and he was a New York icon. Still kind of amazing when you think about it, isn't it? Did he ever have a hit record? Can you name one song that you think of as a "Bobby Short song?" The only one I can think of is the "Charlie" perfume theme that he did in a Revlon commercial back in the mid-1970s.

Compared to Bobby, you might think that DeLorean got Short-changed, but I don't think so. I have no idea how many CEOs of General Motors DeLorean served under during his stay there, but I'd be willing to bet you big bucks that his was a much longer obit than any of them got (or will get.)

And Johnny Cochran? Do you remember where you were when the OJ verdict came in? I sure do (or rather I remember where *I* was). Plus the fact that earlier in this e-mail I used the phrase "race card," which I doubt I would have even known if Johnny hadn't been in the game. On the basis of his contribution to the language alone I think he deserves his 1600.

And that brings us to Robert Creeley. The obit called him "one of the great American poets of the last half-century." I guess the slight 260-word tribute is an indication of how far poetry has disappeared from mainstream culture. Is that a bad thing? I'm not so sure it is. I guess I've always been a believer in the fact that culture has to earn its way to our attention. I will also admit to the fact that last year I read a Creeley collection (1950-1960 poems) and was only intermittently interested.

As you point out, famously he said: drive he sd

And someone made a movie – kind of an art film, if I recall – using that Creeley line as the title. Some people may remember that film, or even that line, but how many millions more remember the Johnny Cochran rhymed couplet: "If the glove doesn't fit / you must acquit"?

260 words for Creeley? About right, I'd say.

Terry.

April 2, 2005 – Gilbert

Terry.

Comedian Mitch Hedberg died at the age of 37 of a heart attack. "I used to do drugs," went one of his most quoted jokes. "I still do drugs. But I used to, too."

He also had problems with alcohol.

My drug and alcohol life came to a halt when I was 34. I am very lucky to be alive, given the degree to which I traveled that dark and lonely highway. People say that writers who drink a lot, like so many do and did, drink because of what they see. But I (and your father, whose definitive writing about Malcolm Lowry's *Under the Volcano* and alcoholism so searingly illuminates) know different. I know that the drinking is what creates the dark side that shows up in the writing (and living) and not the other way around.

For example Hedberg was said to suffer great stage fright. Some said it might have been the cause of a lot of his drug use. Wrong. Drugs and alcohol cause stage fright. I know. They damage the nervous system to hell! So you can't have any inner peace anytime anywhere, but most especially when a whole room full of people are staring right at you.

s.

4 April 2005 – San Miguel de Allende, GTO, MX

steve.

I've gone on at length on the difficulties I have following obituaries down here in San Miguel. If it weren't for the *NYT* on-line I'd certainly have a tough time holding up my end of this correspondence. The *Mexican Miami Herald* simply doesn't cover death the way I've grown to love with the *Times*.

This week, however, it's been quite another story. Death has dominated the front page every day for the last week or so with the real-time dramas of the deaths of Terri Schiavo and the Pope.

I can't remember more public deaths, can you?

Bubbling away in the background, of course, is the impending death of Prince Rainer III. You can tell John Paul II's and the Prince's are major deaths because they have Roman numerals after their names.

I remember clearly the headline in the *Toronto Star* 26 years ago when John Paul II was named Pope. There had been a schism in the College of Cardinals about who should be John Paul I's successor. (One never uses the word "schism" unless one is talking about the Papacy.) The decision was taking longer than usual. The story was that they were trying to decide between one Cardinal who was considered fairly bookish and academic and the eventual John Paul II who was thought of as more of a populist. When the decision was finally reached, the *Star* announced it with the headline: "A Pope for the Masses." I just want to know what editor was looking the other way when someone slipped that one through the cracks.

Terri Schiavo? I put a question mark there because I really don't get all the ballyhoo. I mean it's not just the conservatives who were lined up in favor of throwing her a bone – or a liquefied bone or however they do that in this high tech era. It was also liberals like Jesse Jackson. I gotta tell you I really don't have much time for any of those Jacksons – Jesse or Michael. To be honest Shoeless Joe was really the last of the Jackson boys I had any real emotional connection with.

I know that Jesse Jackson has these impeccable liberal credentials so I should be agreeing with everything he says, but the fact is if it came down to a shoot-out between Jesse and, say, Stonewall, well, I'd have to be behind the stone wall. My problem with Jesse – and I fully acknowledge that this is a foolish prejudice on my part – is that he is just too dumb.

I especially hate it when he comes forward to speak for a point of view I favor. After hearing him speak for a few minutes in the faux-MLK, rising-and-falling cadences I invariably find myself changing my previously deeply-felt position, so great is his reverse power of persuasion for me. This guy couldn't carry his great-great-grandfather Andrew's jock.

Actually – all this ranting aside – I'd be quite interested in Kathy's pov on this. I know that she's approximately 37 times more knowledgeable about God and what he's up to at any given moment than either of us is because we've kind of lost touch. (Or at least I have.) Maybe it's time for her to make a guest appearance in this correspondence. I don't suggest that this be a regular thing – no, no

I strongly object to any practice that would substantially cut into my unbridled opinion time – but as long as this whole thing's about death, I'd be interested in hearing an intelligent Catholic weigh in on the Schiavo case.

t.

5 APRIL 2005 Gilbert. Az.

Ter.

I speak I think for all the lunatic right wing when I say WELCOME to our side on the matter of Jesse Jackson.

Japan's oldest woman, 114-year-old Ura Koyama, died yesterday of pneumonia at a hospital in southern Japan. Japan ranks among nations with the world's longest life spans. In 2003, Japanese women set a new record for life expectancy, at 85.3 years, while men could expect to live 78.3 years.

Experts say a traditional fish-based, low-fat diet is Japan's secret to long life. More convincing than the statistics in Japan is "The China Study," which conclusively demonstrates the link between nutrition and heart disease, diabetes, and cancer.

Referred to as the "Grand Prix of epidemiology" by the *New York Times*, this study examined more than 350 variables of health and nutrition with surveys from 6,500 adults across rural China and Taiwan. While revealing that proper nutrition has a dramatic effect on reducing and reversing these ailments as well as obesity, this study also calls into question the practices of many of the current dietary programs, such as the Atkins diet, that enjoy widespread popularity in the West.

You get thinner for a while, but you die. Is the downside. As Atkins himself did. He died early, all bloated and sick. Fresh fruits and vegetables keep you alive longer and disease-free while you live.

s.

6 April 2005 gilbert az

t.

Piano players live long lives. Have you noticed that? And drummers die young. Recent obits prove this time and time again. There is a reason for this. Drumming is menial like housework compared to two hands playing chords and melodic runs simultaneously.

The reason is hinted at here, oh you poor drummers: A major study of nuns at a convent in Mankato, Minnesota, has discovered that the brain retains the capacity to change and grow stronger even in elderly people. The nuns at this convent regularly live well past 90. Yet they do not suffer from dementia, Alzheimer's or other debilitating brain diseases as early or as severely as the general population. David Snowdon, the University of Kentucky professor who has been studying the nuns for several years, has found that those who earn college degrees, who teach and who constantly challenge their minds live longer than less educated nuns who clean rooms or work in the kitchen. Nuns who drum die young. The beat does not go on.

Brain exercising is a way of life at the nunnery, where the sisters live by the principle that an idle mind is the devil's playground. They write spiritual meditations in their journals and letters to their congressmen and do puzzles of all sorts. Current events seminars are held every week. Raised before television, the nuns are more adept at answering questions on Jeopardy than are the actual contestants.

Most of the nuns at Mankato donate their brains to science upon their deaths. Each neuron in the brain has appendages called axons, which send signals to other nearby neurons. At the other end of the neuron are appendages called dendrites, which receive these messages. Generally, these appendages atrophy with age, but not so in the brains of the Mankato nuns. Researchers have found that intellectual stimulation can spur neuron dendrites to branch out like the roots of growing trees, creating networks of new connections. Like the power grid of an electric company, the branching and connections provide surplus capacity in a brown-out. Thus, when hit by Alzheimer's or by a stroke, a brain with a highly developed set of connections can essentially re-route the circuits and will function far better than a brain that is not so developed.

Writing this very book may be the thing that keeps us alive to write another! So here's a great quote from Nabokov that ties to all this: "It is because you did not like my first book that you have forced me to write a second one."

Steve.

9 april 2005 – San Miguel

steve.

Okay, let's see what we can do with piano players. Do you know who Frank Conroy is … was? He died a few days ago. This prompted the *NYT* to give him a heavy-hitter-like 1100-word obit. I really wonder what percentage of the *NYT* readership has ever heard of him. My best guess: less than 1%.

I actually know about him. Because, for some reason (maybe some brilliant *NYT* review), I read one of his books. It was called *Midair* – a collection of short stories. I thought it was okay. Not great but okay.

Anyway, reading the obit in the *Times* (which tended to go a bit too heavily into literary criticism I thought), I was struck by the fact that for some time Conroy basically earned his living as a piano player. And yet he died at a mere 69. So maybe one has to be a *full-time* piano man to cash in on the piano-player longevity bonus.

Saul Bellow, on the other hand, who to my knowledge did *not* play the piano, lived on to 89. I know you must have been a Bellow fan because at one point you sent me a copy of one of his last books – a novella really – that you had much enjoyed.

The first Bellow book I ever read was *Humboldt's Gift*. Still one of the best books I've ever read. This was, of course, a bit late in the game for discovering Bellow. He was already very well established by the time he got to *Humboldt*. In fact, within a year after *Humboldt* came out, Bellow was awarded the Nobel Prize.

If you haven't read the book, let me tell you that it opens with a funeral and it closes with a funeral. Trudi read the book at about the same time I did. (It was that month's assignment for a book club we belonged to.) She thought the book was about death. I hadn't thought of that, but after she floated the idea, I had to agree it certainly made a lot of sense. Especially given the way funerals start and end the book.

But she further lobbed in the theory that it was *Humboldt's Gift* that tipped the scale that gave him the Nobel. Her point was that in order to win the Big One, you had to have tackled the major literary and philosophical themes. And while the list of exactly what those themes are may vary from one person to another, it's a pretty safe bet that Death would appear on virtually all of them.

This is, of course, why I suggested this book. I thought it high time that we get our Nobel credentials in order. I mean you can just hear the committee discussing your candidacy:

"I certainly agree that *100 Ways to Motivate Yourself* is a classic. But it's a minor classic. Motivation simply isn't one of the big themes."

"What about *The Ten Commitments*?"

"Once again, ground-breaking. But don't be fooled by the biblical sounding title – it's still not about a major theme."

"Well, you have to admit Chandler took on Revenge, and Good and Evil plus the Collapse of the Arizona Diamondbacks in *Two Guys Read Moby-Dick*."

"True enough, but was that Chandler tackling those themes? Or was it Chandler *commenting* on Melville tackling the Diamondbacks' Fall from Grace?"

"Okay, but I hear he's now working on *Two Guys Read the Obituaries*. He pursues Death in all its forms."

"If this is true, then we have no choice but to give it to him! Write the check!"

Now before you say, "Oh, who needs the Nobel Prize anyway?" don't forget that it comes with about $900,000. You could get a nice suit and take Kathy out for a flashy restaurant dinner for that. So don't just blow it off.

t.

12 April 2005 —- Gilbert Az

terry.

I'm writing to you as I sit down to breakfast.

Bellow's best books are *Ravelstein* and *The Actual.* In my opinion. And isn't it interesting that we refer to dead writers in the present tense? Bellow's best books *are.* In Humboldt he *writes* about death. Or, as another example, if I were to quote from your father's book on baseball, I might say, "Here's what your father *says* about the minor leagues..." or something like that as if he were still alive.

And so, as I enjoy breakfast this morning it is not Saul Bellow or the Pope that I mourn but rather Hunter S. Thompson, still, though he died weeks ago. At breakfast, especially. Here's what Thompson says about breakfast, "Breakfast is a personal ritual that can only be properly observed alone, and in the spirit of genuine excess. The food factor should always be massive: four Bloody Marys, two grapefruits, a pot of coffee, Rangoon crepes, a half pound of either sausage, bacon or corned beef hash with diced chilies, a Spanish omelet or eggs Benedict, a quart of milk, a chopped lemon for random seasoning, and something like a slice of Key lime pie, two margaritas and six lines of the best cocaine for dessert...Right, and there should also be two or three newspapers, all mail and messages, a telephone, a notebook for planning the next twenty four hours and at least one source of good music...All of which should be dealt with outside, in the warmth of a hot sun, preferably stone naked."

And I think if more people took his advice, we'd have a better planet. Many of our over-population problems would be solved, for example.

s.

12 april 2005 – SMA

steve.

I am afraid I am not so out-sized in my breakfasts. Fact is I rarely have anything but coffee and a newspaper. However, Thompson makes one suggestion that I totally agree with. He says breakfast should be "outside, in the warmth of a hot sun."

The problem with that, of course, is that opportunity simply doesn't present itself in New York on a year-round basis. Which is why we just bought a house down here. It ups the chances of an outdoor breakfast from about 30% to about 95%. Moving on …

So I was reading Galileo the other day. (Okay, you caught me. I was hoping I could just drift that one past you.) So I was reading a book that happened to *mention* Galileo the other day. It quoted him as saying, "Measure what can be measured and make measurable what cannot be measured."

For the record, today was the 167th straight day that I've written for at least an hour. Cal Ripken is shaking.

Anyway, I believe in measuring things and I know you do too. Does this stem from our childhood fascination with sports and the statistics that measure them? Or is it a natural inclination? A bit of both I suppose. Even when the measurements and statistics offer up no real conclusions, I still find them interesting. So bear with me and consider the word counts on these *New York Times* obits:

• Marius Russo (aged 90; a 1940s Yankee pitcher with a lifetime 45-34 record) – 380 words.

• Prince Rainier – 730 words (Want to venture a guess as to how many he'd have had if he hadn't married Grace Kelly?)

• Edward Bronfman (in the early 1990s one of the richest men in the world; he and his brother controlled an empire worth $80 billion – and back in 1990, that was real money) – 580 words.

• Frank Conway (the writer/piano player I mentioned last time) – 1100 words.

• Saul Bellow (five wives, three national book awards, one Pulitzer and the Nobel) – 3500 words.

And what can we learn from all these numbers (outside of the fact that Saul Bellow knew whereof he spoke when he announced that being a writer is an aphrodisiac)? I think that Bronfman's relatively stingy obit suggests that businessmen get a little undervalued. You'll recall I earlier said that maybe DeLorean got a little under-inked in his obit. To be truthful, this doesn't really bother me. I think it's clear that successful businessmen get more than enough rewards in the here and now for me to be worried about the relative paucity of words they get after death.

The interesting thing is that I think businesspeople get more ink when they've crossed the line that separates the legal from the ill- a bit (or outrageously). For instance, a good part of DeLorean's obit concerned his various trials for cocaine dealing and corporate malfeasance. Imagine how much ink Martha Stewart would get.

But poor Edward Bronfman played by the rules and as a result he gets only a couple hundred more words than a pitcher with 45 lifetime wins.

Terry.

14 April 2005
gilbert az

terry.

Johnnie Johnson, the blues and early rock 'n' roll *pianist* who played on many of Chuck Berry's early hits and performed with Mr. Berry for more than 20 years, died yesterday at home in St. Louis. *He was 80.* His two greatest influences were Earl "Fatha" Hines, a pianist who lived 80 years, and Meade Lux Lewis, a pianist who was headed for a long life when he was killed in a car crash at the age of 59. Jerry Lee Lewis, one of the human body's greatest abusers of all time, is a pianist and still lives today at the age of 70.

Former Crowded House and Split Enz *drummer* and TV personality Paul Hester committed suicide on Saturday after a long battle with depression. *He was 46.*

Spencer Dryden, *drummer* with rock group Jefferson Airplane in the group's heyday of the late 1960s, has died. *Dryden was 66.*

Keith Knudsen, the longtime Doobie Brothers *drummer* who was part of the band during a string of hits that included "Taking it to the Streets" and "Black Water," died of pneumonia Tuesday. *He was 56.*

This is so clear.

s.

U.S. Income Tax Day – 2005

Steve,

You act as if you discovered the drummer-death quirk. Hello! This has been common knowledge and pretty much established as a scientific fact for years. So much so, in fact, that the mockumentary *This is Spinal Tap* made the deaths of the band's various drummers a running gag throughout the movie.

t.

19.4.05 – San Miguel de Allende

Steve.

You see ballplayer obituaries quite frequently and I am almost always interested, whether the player was before my time or not – and, of course, fewer and fewer of them are nowadays. However, the one the other day on Don Blasingame really quite got to me. I'm not really sure why. It wasn't as if I was a huge fan of his. And, as I'm sure he would admit, it's not as if he were one of the greats. But this wave of nostalgia hit me like a moderate-sized tsunami when I saw his name.

Was it because he was a second baseman and *I* was a second baseman at the time? (Albeit in different leagues.) Was I more aware of him because he was a Cardinal and you were – for some reason – a Cardinal fan in those days? (Why *were* you a Cardinal fan, by the way?) I'm sure I haven't spent a lot of time thinking about him the last few years, but somehow he just seemed so much a symbol of a certain period of my life.

There were also a couple of interesting things about the obituary itself. I saw it on-line in the *New York Times*, but it was picked up from the Associated Press. And where did it come from? It was a release from the Hanshin Tigers baseball team in Western Japan, a team Blasingame managed for two years.

It turns out that after Blasingame's career in the U.S. came to an end after 12 seasons and a lifetime .258 batting average, he moved on to Japan where he played, then coached and finally managed for another 16 years! This is not like a lot of those guys who go play in Japan for a year or two in an effort to get picked up again in the U.S. major leagues. Blasingame actually based himself in Japan for more than a fifth of his life. He must have enjoyed it.

Anyway. I know all of this is probably old news to you because I vaguely remember you mentioning that you had actually met him or his son at some point in Arizona. (The obit points out that he died in Fountain Hills, Arizona. Anywhere near you?) But let me ask you if you had ever heard of the Hanshin Tigers? I had!

———

I think I told you that while we were living in Paris I took an intensive French course for three months. It went from 9am to 1pm on weekdays. I used to leave the class each day drained of energy from the effort of concentrating on French that hard for that long. Every two weeks the class would alter somewhat with new students coming in, others leaving. But at any given time, I was generally pretty much the oldest person in the class. I was 55 at the time and the rest of the students were usually between the ages of 18 and 30. I found it very fun and by the mere facts of my age and that there were very few Americans at the school, I had a certain celebrity status, which I quite lapped up.

Anyway at one point there was this Japanese kid in the class – Makio Takenaka. He was in grad school in England (so his English was quite passable, though sometimes I had a hard time understanding him). He befriended me and at some point near the end of our two weeks together we discovered that we were both big baseball fans. I told him that even though I rooted for the Yankees when I was in New York, my favorite team was the Detroit Tigers. He found that amazing because his favorite team was the Hanshin *Tigers*. Both teams were in last place in their respective leagues. They pretty much remained so for the next few years until Hanshin had a breakout season a couple of years ago. I'm expecting Detroit to do the same this year.

I think my favorite team in the Japanese League would have to be the Hiroshima Carp. This is a team that Blasingame managed two different times, but regardless of the Blasingame factor, a great name, don't you think?

terry

25 April 2005 – PHX, AZ

Ter

I too was sad to see that Don Blasingame had died. I used to love the Cardinals, because they were my father's favorite team when I grew up, and Blasingame was the fine young player, never great but always good, who represented transition from the Stan Musial days to the Ken Boyer days.

His cousin Jim Blasingame has become a friend of mine over the years. He hosts a syndicated business radio show.

You and I lived through these baseball players when we were young, and not only followed the leagues they played in but put them into leagues of our own, a groundbreaking concept foreshadowing today's fantasy leagues.

One kid in our school, Hugh Lucas, went further. He created two teams in his own fantasy games made up of kids in our school. One team, the Orange, was made up of kids who were kind to Hugh. (I was on that team.) The other, the Black, was made up of kids mean to Hugh. Or that he despised for other reasons. Those games meant a lot to him. It was awful when the Black won.

———

RE: the Hiroshima Carp.

Still carping about the bomb?
They should have thought of that before they bombed the USS Arizona!

steve.

4 may 2005 – New York City

Steve.

A guy named Gordon Shaw died the other day. He was a physicist and I'm not too proud to confess that I generally skip the obituaries of physicists. But the heading on this one caught my eye: "Gordon Shaw, 72; Tied IQ to Hearing Mozart."

Honest.

Apparently this breakthrough study made big news in the late 1970s when it came out. How did I miss it? Did you know about this? The obit, which gave a capsule summary of the study, said that Beethoven didn't work – it was only Mozart that raised your IQ.

For me it was a very short step to linking this study to the one mentioned earlier in these letters, which demonstrated conclusively that people with high IQs tend to live longer. This linkage leads us directly to the further conclusion that listening to Mozart will increase the length of your life.

Shaw was one of those people the world takes seriously. And yet, how is that possible given what I've just told you about the man? Especially when other scientists at other universities ran the same test and were unable to duplicate the results. And yet the *New York Times* gave him over 500 words.

Did you see that Earl Wilson died? After coming over to the Tigers from the Red Sox in 1967, he won 22 games. In the Tigers' pennant-winning 1968 season, he won another 13 with an ERA under 3.00. Are we the only people in the country that when the name Earl Wilson is brought up, think of the pitcher rather than the columnist?

terry.

6 May 2005

Ter-

Listening to Mozart raises your IQ or suggests your IQ? What happens to my IQ, then, I wonder, when I listen to the Annette Funicello CD you gave me? (As I do quite often.)

s.

8 May 2005 – New York, NY

steve.

I suppose you saw the Derby yesterday. It just goes to show what can happen when you get that many speed horses in a mile-and-a-quarter race. When they posted the time for the first half mile as 45 and change I knew it would be set up for some come-from-behind horse. The pace was simply too fast and predictably it burned out all the colts that got sucked into trying to keep up with Spanish Chestnut.

Someone asked me afterwards why those other horses go after a "rabbit" like that. The problem is that the horses don't know how long the race is. All they have to go on is the jockey's signals. They just know they're in a race and they want to be in front. So, why don't the jockeys hold them back? The belief is that holding them back and having them fight the jockey every stride takes more out of them than chasing a speed horse.

The jockey's supposed to settle the horse into a comfortable position, slip into cruise speed, save ground by not having to go wide around the turns and generally conserve the horse's energy for the stretch run. It's very simple to describe; it's just very, very hard to do.

One of the all-time best at doing just that was Ted Atkinson who died two days before the Derby at 88. He was one of the big jockeys when I was first getting interested in horse racing when I was ten or twelve years old. He was most famous as Tom Fool's jockey. A lot of people believe Tom Fool was one of the top horses of all time. He was Horse of the Year in 1953 as a 4-year-old when he won all ten of his races. This is much harder than winning ten out of ten as a 2- or 3-year-old because at the younger ages weight is assigned by a formula based on the horse's age, sex and the distance. So, for instance, in the Kentucky Derby all colts carry the same 126 pounds.

In your 4-year-old year, however, all the big races are called handicaps. In a handicap the weights are assigned by the track and they are designed to "handicap" the best horses. The better you are, the more weight you'll have to carry. Now I don't have the statistics in front of me, but I guarantee you – especially after Tom Fool's winning streak was well under way – that he would have been giving away 25 to 30 pounds to some of the horses he was running against – and he still beat them. Atkinson rode him on every race he ran.

He obviously made a big impression on Marianne Moore. I include one of her poems called "Tom Fool at Jamaica." A couple of pre-footnotes before you read it: 1) in the '50s, Jamaica used to be the third track in the New York circuit until it was replaced by Aqueduct, and 2) Fred Capossela was the track announcer in New York for years. After that, I don't know what to tell you. Marianne is kind of a difficult poet – jazzy, often obscure and stream-of-consciousy – but I've always kind of liked her. Strange, because usually I don't like obscurity in poetry.

You figure it out:

Tom Fool at Jamaica

Look at Jonah embarking from Joppa, deterred by
the whale; hard going for a statesman whom nothing could
  detain,
although one who would not rather die than repent.
Be infallible at your peril, for your system will fail,
and select as a model the schoolboy in Spain

who at the age of six, portrayed a mule and jockey
who had pulled up for a snail.
"There is submerged magnificence," as Victor Hugo
said, "*Sentir avec ardeur,*" that's it; magnetized by feeling.
Tom Fool "makes an effort and makes it oftener
than the rest"—out on April first, a day of some significance
in the ambiguous sense—the smiling
Master Atkinson's choice, with that mark of a champion, the
        extra
spurt when needed. Yes, yes. "Chance
is a regrettable impurity"; like Tom Fool's
left white hind foot—an unconformity; though judging by
results, a kind of cottontail to give him confidence.
Up in the cupola comparing speeds, Signor Capossela
        keeps his head.
"It's tough," he said; "but I get 'em; and why shouldn't I?
I'm relaxed, I'm confident, and I don't bet." Sensational. He
        does not
bet on his animated
valentines—his pink and black-striped, sashed or dotted
        silks.
Tom Fool is "a handy horse," with a chiseled foot. You've the
        best
of a dancer to a measure or harmonious rush
of a porpoise at the prow where the racers all win easily—
like centaurs' legs in tune, as when kettledrums compete;
nose rigid and suede nostrils spread, a light left hand on the
        rein,
till
well–this is a rhapsody.
Of course, speaking of champions, there was Fats Waller
with the feather touch, giraffe eyes, and that hand alighting
        in
Ain't Misbehavin'! Ozzie Smith and Eubie Blake
ennoble the atmosphere; you recall the Lipizzan school;
the time Ted Atkinson charged by on Tiger Skin—
no pursuers in sight—cat-loping along. And you may have
seen a monkey
on a greyhound. "But Tom Fool. . .

Terry.

10 may 2005. New York.

Steve.

New Yorkers did not walk around with their usual confidence yesterday. Five obits in the *Times* had shown an average death age of 64. A watercolorist, a stage producer, a labor leader, a lawyer and a math teacher.

64! That's like tomorrow isn't it?

You could feel it all over the city. A listlessness, a down-at-the-mouth-ness. I mean why bother? What's the point if you've only got three score and four and no more?

Obviously someone at the *Times* recognized the paper's responsibility and yesterday's gloom was lifted today when they ran four obits with an average age of 92!! The whole town came alive. Even the weather brightened today – sunny and warm.

I really do think that the paper should reexamine their policy and in the future they should simply ignore the deaths of anyone under the age of 60. (60 is an arbitrarily selected age. I swear it's merely a coincidence that it also happens to be ours.)

Terry.

15 May 2005 – Gilbert, AZ.

Ter.

James and Alice Lewis, who were owners and trainers of racehorses together, died eight days apart, race officials said. They were 83. James Lewis died on Tuesday of heart and kidney failure, and his wife died of heart failure on May 2, the officials said. The couple, married 57 years, were rarely seen without each other.

This supports a longstanding theory of mine and others that *purpose* is a major factor in keeping a person alive. James and Alice were, in many ways, living for each other for 57 years, and when one died so did the other.

So goals and purpose are a big factor. Also, letting go of the Bible's three score and ten. That helps. Just forget that erroneous mythology. Remember that the Bible makes no mention of the dinosaurs. Quite an oversight! So why cling to its "science" in other areas? You'll live longer if you don't.

I think your last note on NOT running deaths 60 and under in the obits was brilliant. Or maybe even run them as Accidental and Untimely. We hear quite often about untimely deaths, that's why I was pleased to see that most of the major news media were referring to the Pope's "timely" death last month.

s.

21.5.05 – NYC, NY

Steve.

After a week that featured a day with only a 64-year-old average death in the *New York Times* followed immediately by a day with a 92-year average, the paper produced the strangest one of all – a no-obit day!

It was the very first non-obituary day in my memory. Now what could that mean? Was it serendipity or policy?

In the past I had believed that it was a *Times* rule that there would be at least one obit every day. I figured this rule was based on a feeling that it was generally unwise to allow people to believe in immortality. For the most part I would tend to agree with this. Things get out of hand when people feel they will live forever – witness the behavior of people in their twenties.

But if the *New York Times* can toss away death as a passing fad like an outmoded typeface or a hula-hoop, then can taxes be far behind? Yes, as the conservative press has long complained, the *Times* has way too much power.

t.

25-05-05 – new york, new york 10012

steve.

A 92-year-old average on three obits in the *Times* yesterday, and a 91-year average on another three today. I'm liking this trend.

Included today was the voice of "Tony the Tiger." Thurl Ravencroft was from Nebraska, and like all the rest of us who grew up in the Midwest and who had ambitions, he left as soon as he could. Nowadays, of course, the voices for animated characters in movies are all done by major Hollywood stars. But in those days, there were people who did nothing but voice-overs and cartoon voices. Thurl created the "Tony the Tiger" voice and for more than 50 years was the man who said the "Grrrreeat!" that I bet you can hear in your mind as you read this.

He claimed to be the only man in the world that made his career with one word. (I'll bet the guy who does "AFLAC!" has set his sights on that too.) Tony the Tiger, dead at 91.

Reading about this reminded me of the advertising agency that created that Frosted Flakes campaign – Leo Burnett in Chicago. They were famous for creating these personifications of their clients' products and then putting a lot of money behind the advertising for them. The Jolly Green Giant. The Pillsbury Doughboy. Tony the Tiger. The Marlboro Man. I think all of those were Leo Burnett campaigns.

When I was starting in advertising, the guys I worked with at Y&R all had to acknowledge the effectiveness of these campaigns, but I don't think any of us aspired to creating them. We looked more to the hipper, edgier stuff that was coming out of the hot agencies in New York rather than turning to Chicago for our model.

Of course now these Burnett campaigns seem very old-fashioned, reminders of those hazily innocent days of our youth. I wonder what Leo would have made of the Nike stuff.

I still think cartoon characters are basically silly. They just don't interest me. Not just in advertising, but on television shows and in movies too. I've never seen a single *Simpsons* episode. *South Park* either. Though I have seen pieces of each. And I really deplore animated films taking up valuable screen space in Cineplexes throughout the country. Miranda is a big fan of the *Shrek* and *Toy Story* films and has gotten me to see one of each, but that's it. I was bored by them. In fact, the only time I saw a lot of animated films was when Lincoln and Andrew were kids.

Is there something wrong with me?

terry

5-26-05 – NYC

Steve.

Ismail Merchant. At only 68.

Who can say Merchant without Ivory in these days? And yet it never crossed my mind until I read the obit that they were lovers. Did you know/suspect this? The obit made it fairly clear.

The obit also ran through a list of their films and it struck me – not for the first time – that I don't understand how a director (or in this case a producer/director team) can make a good film, one that I very much like, and then turn around and make a film I hate.

I loved *The Remains of the Day*. How could the same people that made that film make *Jefferson in Paris*? Did you see that? Nick Nolte as Tom Jefferson? Very, very bad.

Just as writing is basically just telling a story, directing is simply telling a story on film. The *way* you tell the story is your style. But with writers, (okay, there are certainly some exceptions, but generally …) if I like the way the writer tells a story, I tend to like all his/her books. I like every book Jane Austen wrote; I like every book that Anthony Powell wrote; I like every book A.J. Liebling wrote; and every book Mordecai Richler wrote. I certainly will like some better than others, but all of those writers' books will fall on the "like" rather than the "dislike" side of the equation. I am surprised the same does not follow with directors.

Or am I?

The problem with film is that one person's vision doesn't shape the product. It's all collaborative. I learned this making television commercials all those years. The modern age loves this kind of thing. It loves interdependence. It loves "reaching out" to other people.

I no longer want to.

As I typed that last sentence I realize that this is a bit of a lie. The fact is: I *never* wanted to.

To me art is the manifestation of one person's unique point-of-view. A Picasso *is* Picasso. Or *Brideshead Revisited is* Waugh. But *Jefferson in Paris* is Merchant, Ivory, Nolte, Paltrow, James Earl Jones, Greta Scacchi, the cameraman and on and on. That's not art as I see it. That's merely a business partnership. Of course I love film, it's merely that I don't really consider it an art form. This is not a commonly held belief these days, but I really think art is the great showcase for the individual. People talk about "collaborative art," which I see as an absolute contradiction in terms.

I know everyone says that it's the director's vision that informs the film, and I'm willing to grant that the director probably has more to say about how it comes out than anyone, but it simply isn't totally in his control. Anyway, I bet that lack of total control is the reason that in a list of any director's films I will love some and hate others.

Where are you on film as art? Or does it even matter?

Terry.

27 May 2005

Terry-

I think you're right about movies not being art. Because, as you say, it's art by committee. Which is silly. Of course, your theory rules this book out. As being thought of as art. Somehow, that disturbs me.

steve

28 May 2005 – NYC

Steve.

A couple of interesting obits today. Eddie Albert at 99. Another boy from the Midwest who got out early. He had been the warden in the first *The Longest Yard*. He died the day before the release of the re-make. By the way, when you get into your late-90s or early-100s, be sure to watch out for pneumonia, it seems to get them every time at that age.

But the obit that prompted me to write was Chico Carrasquel, 77. When I first started following baseball, Chico was the prototypical great-fielding shortstop. He was also, as they pointed out in the obituary, the first Venezuelan star in the majors.

After his sixth season with the White Sox, they traded him to Cleveland. I remember when it happened. It seemed so strange to me that they'd do that, trade away the best fielding shortstop in the majors. Of course, they knew what I didn't, which was that they had a replacement for him in the minors. Another slick-fielding Venezuelan – Luis Aparicio.

I just looked Aparicio up and discovered that he led the American League in stolen bases nine years in a row. The first time in his rookie year, he stole 21. Also, Aparicio played 2599 games and never played a single inning at any other position than shortstop. I wonder if he's still alive.

t.

29 May 2005
gilbert

terry

I love your daily calculations on the average age of death of people in the obits, using it as a predictor of your own death, or should I say of *our* death, since we are the same age.

Why do we want to live as long as possible? That's my question. Most people who see people in their 90s say, "I wouldn't want a life like that. I wouldn't want to live that long."

Is it that we have not accomplished enough and we need more time to do this? Have you not just won a prize and a reading for your play, *Hamlet - The Sequel*? (A very funny play, reminding me of Woody Allen's early plays.) So why would you need more than that?

I love your reference to the immortal, infinite day on which there were no obituaries. Recently the *NYTimes* ran a nice story on Stanley Kunitz, two-time American poet laureate who is nearly 100 years old and still writing and still actively tending his garden. Kunitz says he has become reconciled to death by realizing "that death is absolutely essential for the survival of life itself on the planet; the earth would become full of old wrecks." Kunitz then says, "Immortality? It's not anything I'd lose sleep over."

Here's the problem with accomplishment and achievement. It's empty. Who cares, in the end? If you accomplish a lot, you'll only be resented by future generations who have to study you. You'll be hated for it! Look at Melville! Look at Chaucer. Look at James Madison!

I think you made a good point about art and whether movies are art (because of the collaborative nature.) Was Billy Wilder an artist? Was Ingmar Bergman or Fellini? They would say yes. You would say no. I would say yes but with an asterisk, like Maris, and like the steroid asterisk by Barry Bonds' name in the record books. The director asterisk would say "team effort."

Death gives us life. But we don't think of it that way. We are pretty negative about death ... the very thing that gives us life, in the same way that heads gives us tails and Pat Boone gives us Elvis.

Elvis died young after finding out that fame means nothing at all. He would have been happier driving that truck. He'd be alive today with lots of kids and grandkids and an old guitar he always plays at family gatherings. ("Play 'Old Shep,' Grandpa!").

Fame itself doesn't ruin a life or foreshorten it, is my theory, but rather it is the crashing disappointment fame brings. Disappointment and depression and drugs are what a lot of people call the effects of "fame." But they are part of the disappointment. You think you will have "made it" but no one ever makes it that way. Look at F. Scott Fitzgerald. A truly great writer who, like Dylan Thomas, wasted it all partying. Death in a bottle. Or as Dylan Thomas's wife called it, "Leftover life to kill."

As to your remarks about the death of Chico Carrasquel, I had not known that Venezuela was so dear to your heart. You learn things about your friends every day.

Merchant and Ivory didn't do *Goldfinger*, did they? If you spray your body with gold paint, you can die. Because your cells can't die and leave. They stay. Your body needs cell death to live. And so does the body we know as the universe. It thrives on death. Just as heads thrives on tails. Day thrives on night. Life thrives on death, yet, yet...we furiously calculate the average age of those dying in today's *NYTimes* obit. (I do it too!....90? YES! 85? Okay. 63? Oh no.)

What shall we do with all these years we're hoping for? I'm going to try to finish the work that Dylan Thomas and Fitzgerald did not choose to finish. (Poor me, poor me, pour me another! I told

Kathy yesterday that, for a joke, I wanted Warren Zevon's "Poor Poor Pitiful Me" played at my funeral. Just to shake up the crowd. To weird them out.)

I could try to achieve that. (And I plan to.) Or what if I focused instead on this next fresh moment? What if I cared nothing for the future and believed, as Nabokov believed, that *the future doesn't exist*. Would we still have a book?

s.

30 May 2005 – New York

steve.

Gee, Steve, you've gone all metaphysical on me. All that stuff about how opposites need each other.

But I was certainly glad to hear from you after a bit of a drought. I thought maybe you were down on death the way so many others seem to be.

Your theory about fame not shortening a life, but rather the letdown that follows fame being the culprit reminds me of a Casey Stengel story.

He was asked by a reporter if he believed that having sex the night before a game had a detrimental effect on a player's performance. No, he said, *having* sex did not hurt performance; it was *looking* for sex the night before a game that was the problem.

I am now going to be giving some serious thought to what song I want played at my funeral. Your bringing it up reminded me that I haven't given it a moment's thought until now. But don't worry, I'm on it.

"It's My Party and I'll Cry if I Want to"? That's just a first thought.

t.

30 May 2005
gilbert

ter

I know you think I'm going metaphysical, but there's a reason. Metaphysical practices lead to a fuller and longer life. I can actually verify this for you, but for the short version, let's just look at the death, today, of a man I admired tremendously, Martin Lings.

Lings was a widely acclaimed British scholar whose books on Islamic philosophy, mysticism and art reflected his own deep belief in Sufism, the esoteric, purely spiritual dimension of Islam. He died at his home in England. He was 96.

Ninety-six!

steve.

31 May 2005 – NYC

steve.

I had vaguely noted the obituary of someone named Lings in the *Times*, but had not paid attention since I had no idea who he was. Plus, for me, an obit headed "a Sufi Writer on Islamic Ideas" just ain't a grabber.

Anyway, your saying you admired the guy sent me back to the *Times* to read it – this time on the internet since I'd already thrown the paper away.

I earlier had the impression that the guy was some kind of mystic. I must admit, I don't understand mystics. More than that, I don't understand how they're able to get jobs or how they're able to pull the wool over so many people's eyes. I suppose it's all about needing to believe – you think? My question is do *they* believe? Or are mystics pretty much in the tradition of those television evangelists who seem to believe only in money and their own infallibility?

All of these random and gratuitous thoughts lost their edge when I finally read the obit and discovered that Lings was not a mystic at all; he was actually just an academic. Obviously a pretty good one. What was it you admired in him? I mean besides the very admirable 96-year death age.

But while there in the *Times* obit section on-line I got lured into reading Rita Hayworth's obituary from 1987. You know they have that sort of "Golden Oldies" section on-line where they have obits from years past.

I had not realized Rita suffered from Alzheimer's from a relatively early age. At the age of 50 she was cast in a Broadway play but had to be removed because she could not remember her lines. Still she managed to process five husbands before she could no longer remember their names.

We're going back down to Mexico tomorrow. A lot of house things to do. Adios.

t.

2 June 2005
gilbert

terry.

You have not read my book *Ten Commitments* yet but you will notice when you do that I write about a link I see between the profession of acting and the metaphysical. You also noted that I went metaphysical on you a message or two ago, then I followed up with my admiration of Martin Lings, an astonishingly great man and metaphysical author who died last week at the age of 96.

Ninety-six.

And not too many days earlier we heard that Sir John Mills, Hayley's father and a fine British stage actor, had died at the age of 97. Despite failing health, Mills continued working until the last. Speaking on BBC *Breakfast With Frost* in 2002, Sir John told David Frost he would never retire. "When I get out there, coming across the footlights, it's something that I can hardly explain... such warmth greets me and I feel terrific; it's just wonderful." That corresponds quite nicely with Martin Lings' own huge passion for Sufi spirituality and its history and the active, enthusiastic role he played in getting the Western mind to understand the Sufis.

Ninety-seven.

S.

5 June 2005 – San Miguel de Allende

Steve.

Last year when we came to San Miguel for a vacation and arrived the day before Super Bowl, we received a serendipitous invitation to watch the game at a party. We didn't know anybody at the party when we went, but met a whole bunch of very nice people there and had a terrific time.

This year we arrived in San Miguel again the week of Super Bowl. I called on a friend we had met at that party last year and asked if he wanted to watch the game with us at a local sports bar. He said there was again a Super Bowl party at the same place as last year and after a phone call we were again invited. Once again we watched the Patriots win the game and once again we had a great time with terrific food and good company.

One extremely awkward moment came prior to the game this year when we were working out the details on the betting pool. Now you know that I understand numbers and betting things like this so I volunteered to try to sort it out for them. It was one of those simple 10-across/10-down grid things and I quickly had it ship-shape.

At one point, the guy I had been working with on this said, "Oh, I have a hundred pesos for Bob *[our host, whom I had not seen yet during the afternoon.]*"

"Okay, that's ten squares. How many does Jo *[Bob's wife, whom I had also not yet seen that evening]* want?"

Stunned silence at the betting pool table.

Well, of course Jo was dead. She had died in June. I had to translate this from being told that she had "passed," but I'm very fluent in Euphemism.

Clearly I am very embarrassed by this whole thing (though not sure how I could have avoided it) but with my legendary sunny charm I am able to weather the storm and move on to the game. Once again a Michigan quarterback leads the Pats to victory. Had fun and met a lot of new people, including a guy Miranda talked to for a while who had done the barbecue for the party. I was introduced to him as "Barbecue Bob." Now seriously, Steve, do you want to be known as "Barbecue Steve" for the rest of your life? But, hey, different strokes …

So this story is obviously about death. But what does it have to do with obituaries?!?

———

Fast forward to our return to San Miguel two days ago. We get here on Wednesday but today pick up *Atencion*, the local weekly English language paper, which comes out on Fridays. I turn the page and there is an obituary – sort of a memorial tribute actually – to Barbecue Bob. It was a full spread. He died of a heart attack a week ago.

———

Dear Abby,

Next year I will again be living in San Miguel during the Super Bowl. I suspect I will be invited to the same party. Obviously one person from this party each year is marked for death. Say there will be twenty people at the party. It would then appear to me that my odds of dying in 2006 would be 1 in 20 or 5%. Is this an acceptable risk?

Should I accept the invitation? (It *is* a good party.)

If I don't accept (and keep Miranda away, too), am I then responsible for raising the odds for the people who *do* attend to 1 in 18 or 5.6%?

To absolve myself of this responsibility, should I get two other people to go in our place?

Am I then responsible for their potential deaths?

What if I invite people I don't like to go in our place? What are the ethics of that? Would it be okay if they were essentially evil people, or if I *suspected* them of being evil? What about dull people?

There's no real hurry on this, but please let me know by the time the playoffs are down to the last four teams; I hate to leave a host guessing how many mushroom caps to stuff.

Thank you.

Sincerely,
At A Loss

———

George Mikan died. Now we just missed his playing days. I certainly was aware of him, but I think he retired the year before the Pistons moved from Fort Wayne to Detroit so he was more of a legend than a player by the time we were following the pro game.

Remember Walt Dukes for the Pistons in those early days? He was seven feet tall. I was standing by the tunnel the players went down when they left the court for the locker room at the half and I remember some wit standing next to me saying "How's the weather up there?" when Dukes went by.

Mikan was 6'10", two inches short of Dukes and yet Dukes was just a pretty good center, while Mikan was the most dominant man in the game. Bob Cousy, who was quoted in the obit, said that it was because Mikan was so big and strong. He said that the Celtic center at the time was Ed MacCauley (remember him, "Easy Ed?") at

6'9". He said when you saw him standing next to Mikan, MacCauley looked like a waif even though he was only an inch shorter.

The obit was an eye-opener for me. After reading it, I don't think it's an outrageous statement to credit Mikan with making the game what it is today.

Consider: because Mikan was such a dominant force underneath they put in the 3-second rule. They also had to widen the paint to its current width. But most important, because teams would typically try to beat Mikan by slowing the game down to a standstill (in the obit they cited a game against Ft. Wayne that ended 22-17 or something like that), the league instigated the 24-second clock.

Now outside of the 3-point shot, aren't those the givens that most influence the way the game is played today?

⌁━━━⌁

By the way, last night Miranda and I "watched" game seven of the Pistons/Heat series. We went to a couple of sports bars, but local cable does not carry TNT! No one had the game on TV. Casa Payo, however, has a computer in the corner of the bar that anybody can use for free, so about five of us gathered round it and watched the line-by-line, play-by-play. Very weird. This is how you "see" the game:

1:19	Wade loses the ball to Prince	82-82
0:57	Billups scores on a lay-up	82-84
0:54	Miami Timeout	82-84

Etc. Still, I liked the outcome so I'm not complaining. The finals will be on a real network so all the bars will have them. I am not very sanguine actually about the Pistons' chances against the Spurs, but I am truly impressed by the team.

terry.

7 June 2005

ter.

When you and I were young we loved Chico Carrasquel for being who he was. His essence. We would joke about him, too, because he was not overly impressive to us (nor was anyone else...our humor nailed absolutely everyone including religious icons and leveled the playing field every day).

Today we are serious. And we see significance in everything. This is why WE must die, the sooner the better. That Chico was the first Venezuelan would have meant nothing to us as the happy youth we were, because we did not need to cling to significance as our lives disappeared. We just laughed and enjoyed. He could have been from Puerto Rico or Cuba or Costa Rica or Jamaica or Mexico and what would it have mattered? Nothing.

Studies show that children laugh up to 200 times a day. Grown-ups laugh an average of 12 times. That, to me, explains the necessity of death. If you can't take a joke, go die. That's what God says. He evaluates people by how lightly they take themselves and how seriously they take themselves. It's like Chesterton said, the only reason angels can fly is because they take themselves so lightly.

Don't cry for me, Venezuela.

So all of this is an explanation of my sarcasm, which I was not proud of, my sarcasm that said I didn't know that you cared that much for Venezuela ... that Chico was a Venezuelan and the first Venezuelan to play major league baseball. It wasn't you, it was me. "Wow," I said to myself. "That's significant!" (I was sentencing myself to death.)

Did I say baseball? Baseball! That sport that now mocks itself with Jeff Kent, Tony Womack and Kenny Lofton. Every year they are in a different uniform. Every year. Why don't their agents suit up? It's all about the agents now. Like Seinfeld once said, you don't cheer for the players any more because the players are different every year.

You cheer for the uniform itself. Here come those pinstripes! I stand and cheer. How can you love a team? Not one player wants to play for that team you love. Not one, because off they go next year! I long for the days when I was a radical who hated capitalism. I watched *The Weather Underground* the other night, the documentary about many of my old left-wing heroes from the 60s. You don't need a weatherman to tell which way the wind blows. Where have you gone Joe DiMaggio? A nation turns its lonely eyes to you. (Dylan and Paul Simon actually toured together not long ago. Dylan led with "The Ballad of Chico Carrasquel.")

steve.

8 june 2005 – San Miguel de Allende

Steve.

When I first moved to New York 21 years ago I started reading *The New York Times* on a daily basis. And I discovered every Tuesday they have a section called "Science Times." Originally I would simply toss that entire section, the way I currently do to the weekly automotive section the *Times* has on Sundays. I mean I'm simply not a big science guy (despite the Jens/Saffian training). *[A reference to two junior high science teachers we had.]*

But then every once in a while a headline in one of those science stories would catch my eye and I'd read the thing. After a few years I started actually going through "Science Times" each week. I'm still not a science guy, but every few weeks or so I will find there a fact nugget that makes looking at it each week worth the time.

The fact you cited about children laughing 200 times a day while adults do so only 12 times is exactly the kind of thing I'm talking about. I'll now carry that bit of knowledge around – and quote it occasionally – to the end of my days. Did you pick it up in "Science Times?"

t.

Gilbert, Az. 9 June 2005

Terry.

I think MY end of 2GRTO has gone flat and rather than being lively like *Two Guys Read Moby-Dick*, this book for me has become like Simon and Garfunkel's Old Friends: sit on the park bench like bookends. So I interjected Venezuelan Controversy to compare our laughing youth to frowning, serious adulthood seeking significance and importance.

That's what the fear of death does, it has us falling down the mountain grasping at the little shrubs. That's my theory. Also, people wanted more give and take and back and forth in these books and that's what I'm doing.

It takes a lot of muscles to frown, pondering our identities. This message is posted on a cop's desk at police headquarters in Detroit, and it's an inspiring saying originally said by Norman Vincent Peale:

TOO OFTEN WE LOSE SIGHT OF LIFE'S
SIMPLE PLEASURES. REMEMBER, WHEN
SOMEONE ANNOYS YOU IT TAKES 42 MUSCLES
IN YOUR FACE TO FROWN. BUT IT ONLY
TAKES 4 MUSCLES TO EXTEND YOUR ARM
AND BITCH-SLAP THE MOTHERFUCKER
UPSIDE THE HEAD.

s.

9 june 2005 – San Miguel de Allende

Steve.

Yes, maybe we're getting too bogged down in death. I think we should more often let the obit propel us into orbit. Rather than talk about death all the time – though obviously it is a natural – we should go off on whatever tangent the subject suggests.

⌐━━━┐

I once read a book called *20 Lines A Day* by a writer named Harry Mathews. He apparently has a bit of a reputation as an experimental novelist and he was a good friend of that offbeat European writer, now dead, Georges Perec. Perec was the guy that wrote a novel without using the letter E. Now why would anybody do that? I mean what point is he trying to make?

Anyway, Mathews would sit down to write each day and before he started on his novel or an essay or whatever serious work he had set out for himself, he had to fill a page with twenty lines of writing. He said he started out doing it as a warm-up for his serious stuff, but after a while the 20 lines became a form in itself.

They were sometimes almost diary entries about an incident the previous day. Sometimes they'd be reminiscences. Sometimes almost lyric poetry. Sometimes travel writing. The form was very open in everything but length.

The point I want to make is that he did this for several years and I think the book only included maybe 150. So obviously he edited a lot. You talk about feeling that this is not as lively as our previous book. Well, maybe it isn't; I don't know yet. The fact is I had the very same feeling last year about the Moby-Dick book about half way through it. But I just kept plugging away at it and constantly tried to think of new ways to make it interesting to somebody besides the two of us. It's like doing 20 lines a day. Something good will turn up … or it won't. But you'll never know unless you keep turning 20.

And to the editing point. 2GRMD was about 35,000 words. We've already produced 26,000 words on the obits and we're only in the first third of June. Chances are by the end of the year we'll wind up with raw material of somewhere between 50- and 60-thousand words. So if you think you're turning out dull crap some day, that's terrific, because it will give us something to cut.

Meantime, lighten up. Do you know adults average only 12 smiles a day? Shoot for 13 today!

t.

14 June gilbert

terry,

The poet Richard Eberhart is dead at 101, and I remember seeing and hearing him read his poems at the University of Arizona back when I was a student. He was dignified, understated and in awe of the life force. In his work, anyway. When Richard was 18, his mother died of cancer. Shortly afterward, his father lost his fortune. These experiences, he would later say, helped make him a poet.

This is interesting to me because as you know I write books about this very thing, this very choice we make internally when things go "wrong" whether to see them as having gone "wrong" (mother dead, father loses all) or to let them shake you to your core and then ... and then ... become a poet! God loves this choice, and "Here," said God almighty, "how about I give you 101 years for that?"

Steve

15 june SMA

steve.

A capitalization thing. You wrote "God almighty." Now while intellectually it makes all the sense in the world not to capitalize "almighty," somehow it doesn't look right to me. On the other hand why would a mere adjective be elevated to capitalization just because of its association with God, Who, according to the Associated Press style sheet, does deserve capital status.

⊶⊷

Last night down here we rented *Closer* with Jude "If They Expose a Frame of Film Anywhere in the World I Need to be

There" Law and Clive Owen. When we rented it, my only question was who was going to play Mariano Rivera, whose life story I figured the film was. Imagine my surprise then when there was not even an appearance by Mariano – nor Rollie Fingers nor Sparky Lyle nor Goose Gossage. I felt I'd been duped, but we watched it anyway. It turns out to be all about sex, although there is none in the film.

Not badly done I thought, but the thing that prompts me to bring it up with you is that the character played by Jude Law is an obituary writer for one of the London newspapers and there are a couple of interesting conversations about obits. In one, Jude talks about the euphemistic conventions obituarists employ. Some, of course, we've known about for years.

Reference to X's "very good friend" of the same sex, means X was gay. And his "very good friend" was his lover.

If X died after a "long illness," it used to mean he had cancer. Now, of course, they actually come out and say it. I wonder why cancer was such a taboo subject. In the beginning, AIDS was much the same and you had to read between the lines of the obit to know what the guy died of.

The one Jude mentioned that I guess I'd never thought about was if X was described as "convivial" it meant he was an alcoholic.

t.

gilbert.az.2005.june.16

ter

I notice I put "Gilbert" on all of these, which is home, a little town outside of Phoenix that I have loved living in for years. In fact, looking back over this year of posts to this book so far, I have been in 23 different cities and 11 different states. But travel is the nature of my work as a touring public speaker, shamelessly flying to wherever they will pay money to hear me speak. So though I say "Gilbert," it is almost never really Gilbert, and last week it was

Spartanburg, South Carolina, and next week it is Sun Valley, Idaho, but it saves thought to simply say "Gilbert."

                       ❧━━━━❧

The world's oldest married man has died today at the age of 105. Percy Arrowsmith and his wife Florence, 100, made it into the Guinness Book of Records after celebrating their 80th wedding anniversary on June 1. The couple, from Hereford, UK, also held the record for being the oldest married couple in the world.

News accounts say that "Mr Arrowsmith died peacefully at his home on Wednesday morning."

I've always wondered about that idea of dying peacefully. Dylan Thomas, hating to see his father die, wrote the powerful poem "Do Not Go Gentle Into That Good Night." He did not want his father to die peacefully. Most alcoholics (I used to be one! So I know!) fear death. Really fear death tremendously. Dylan Thomas wrote powerfully about the sway that death had over his thinking. Another of his great poems was "And Death Shall Have No Dominion."

So if I was Dylan's dad, and I wanted to please my son, how would I die? Certainly not like the 105-year-old Percy Arrowsmith. Certainly not peacefully. Or in my sleep. And by the way, how does one know that someone died in his sleep? How do you know that? What if he looked like he was going to sleep, but instead he just closed his eyes to die? You pulled the covers up over him, you opened the window by his bed. You took the book he was reading out of his hands and set it down so he could read it tomorrow, but you didn't know that he was already dead. There would be no tomorrow. "He died in his sleep," you would say.

Here's another scenario I've always wondered about: What if he had fallen asleep, had a dream about being shot, and at the moment he was shot in his dream, he died in reality? Then he did die in his sleep. But in the dream itself, it was really feeling real, really feeling like death itself. And were he alive to talk about it, he would say, "I had this dream that I died and it really, really felt real!"

S.

17 june 2005. SMA

steve.

They say the Arrowsmiths' sex life had gotten to feel pretty routine the last few months. Florence Arrowsmith said "the old spark just wasn't there anymore." That might have had something to do with Percy's demise. Though, once again, one should be cautious about jumping to conclusions about cause and effect.

Whenever people ask me where I grew up I always say "near Detroit." And they always read something in that. And they're always wrong.

They think that I'm saying "near Detroit" because I'm ashamed of Detroit and I want to make it clear that I grew up outside of Detroit. The real reason is the same as why you usually say Phoenix instead of Gilbert. Nobody knows where Gilbert is. Well, nobody knows where Birmingham is either. And even if they say they do, they're usually mentally down in Alabama somewhere about 800 miles off. So I say, "near Detroit."

Why "near?"

Because if somebody does know the Detroit area, they'll ask, "Where near Detroit?" But if I had just said "Detroit," they'd've let it go and I'd miss some major coincidence. Like the time Miranda and I were in a pub in Galway and we struck up a conversation with a young woman who was living in Galway. After I said "near Detroit" she asked where and it turned out she grew up in Birmingham and on Mohegan and used to baby-sit for friends of mine from college.

Meeting young women in bars: Miranda and I met one down here while watching the Pistons game the other night. When Miranda told her I was originally from Michigan, the girl asked me, "Where on the hand are you from?" It is true that all people from

Michigan in any attempt to explain anything about the geography of the state put up their right hand to form a fleshy map of the lower peninsula of the State and then point places of interest out on it with their left hand. Do you still?

t.

23 June 2005

Ter

No I have never raised my hand to describe the shape of Michigan, although I may now start.

As we read these obituaries I am keeping track of certain professions that lead to an early death and certain professions that lengthen life. Drummers, as is well known, especially in the world of rock, don't have long to live. But here is a profession that you really want to avoid. It is the profession of Rain Queen: "Makobo Modjadji, the famed rain queen of South Africa's Balobedu people, has died of unspecified causes." She was 27!

Steve

June 26, 2005 – new york

steve.

Vera Komarkova. Dead at 62.

I bring her up not because I had ever heard of her before or because she seems to have been a superstar in a world I know nothing about (mountaineering), but because she was a woman. All the time now I read about women being honored or having lengthy obits being published about themselves just because they are women.

It's our era, Steve.

But even as I typed the word "era" I was thinking of the "equal rights amendment" rather than era meaning a period of time and this in itself is obviously a tribute to the effect of the women's movement. (Okay, Steve, I know *you* are probably thinking "earned run average," but admit it, your second thought was "equal rights amendment.")

At one point in my life when I was visiting your fair state with Andrew, I had dinner with Fred. I happened to mention that I was having a difficult time figuring out what my then wife Trudi wanted. And that I found it very upsetting. Did she want a career? a family? a good time? – she didn't seem to know. But somehow her not knowing made her very unhappy with me.

Fred, who had just been through a divorce told me that, yes, it was hard. He said he thought the greatest issue of our generation, especially for more-or-less privileged upper middle-class males like us, was the question of "gender." Normally we think of the Viet Nam War or Civil Rights as the leading issues of our time. But when you think about it, "women's rights" in all its various guises has affected us in the way we live every day probably more than any other issue in our lifetime. Fred was absolutely right – it has been the defining issue of our time.

And here comes Vera. Only two years older than we are, Vera is a footnote. She wouldn't even have footnote status if she'd been a man. She climbed the 10th highest mountain in the world! The 10th! And she was far from the first to do it. But the fact is, she was a woman and she was part of a 10-woman mountain climbing team so it was sort of a novelty act. (They even had t-shirts made that said: "A Woman's Place is on Top.")

Seriously, I don't mean to take anything away from her; she was obviously an impressive woman. She got a Ph.D. in biology and she could climb mountains so she's two ahead of me right there. But it all reminds me of a pet peeve of my father's. He said it used to annoy him no end when society would praise a 75- or 80-year-old man for doing something that would have been a commonplace for a 40-year-old. Said he found it condescending.

In Vera's case, it's clear that she wouldn't have even gotten a *NYT* obit if she'd been a *man* with the same resume. This doesn't actually annoy me at all. I just find it interesting as a sign of our times.

Still, even in this time, a woman's lot is a hard one. For instance, some of them are forced to be rain queens. I have never heard of a male rain queen. Any idea of the life expectancy of rain *kings*?

t.

26 June 2005
Gilbert

Dear Terrence

(I notice that you use Terrence as your professional author's name, so I thought I'd do it once in awhile, too, so that readers might know that you really are the same guy, not his younger, wilder son "Terry.")

I would not sign up for rain queen or rain king or prince of precipitation. Given how long they live. I was deeply disturbed yesterday listening to a Tom Peters CD (he's a business management guru) in my car and hearing him say that now that he's 61 years old he has freedom to say whatever he wants at his public speaking gigs because he knows that at that advanced age he's not going to get asked back. What is he thinking? That he's a rain king?

Love to your lovely wife,

s.

27 june 2005 – nyc

steve.

I opened the obits page today and immediately recognized the name of Paul Winchell. Remember him, the ventriloquist? Paul

Winchell and Jerry Mahoney. Maybe you don't, but I do because I had a Jerry Mahoney doll.

I even remember reading in the instruction book that Bs were impossible to say without moving your lips and that ventriloquists had learned the trick of replacing their Bs with Gs. You were told to practice by saying the phrase "a bottle of beer." After that I always noticed ventriloquists when they did their Bs. But the fact is that once you know their trick, it really does sound like "a gottle of geer."

People noticing this is perhaps the cause of the demise of the ventriloquist's art during our brief lifetimes. When we were kids ventriloquists used to be a staple of those general variety entertainment shows like the Ed Sullivan Show. Right off the bat I can name four that were in action at the time: Paul and Jerry, Edgar Bergen and Charlie McCarthy, that guy that used to the Nestles commercials with his dog dummy, and Senor Wences (sp?). Now who would you say is the top ventriloquist going today? Some might say Dick Cheney, but he's really not that funny.

Perhaps ventriloquism is due for a major comeback. I hope not.

The bizarre thing about the obits in the *Times* today was that the heading on the Winchell piece added "And Film Voice of Pooh's Tigger." Right next to this was the obit of John Fiedler (one of those character actors who you recognize immediately but never knew his name) and the second line on the heading of *his* obit said, "And Film Voice of Pooh's Piglet."

It was a sad day for Winnie.

t.

3 july 2005 gilbert az

Terry.

You ask if I have any idea of the life expectancy of rain kings?

Saul Bellow's Henderson will live forever. *Henderson the Rain King* is a wild and energetic novel about a man full of life. And because it is imaginary it lives beyond Bellow's death. I read today that there are 11 parallel dimensions. I imagine one of those has everybody's next novel in it

I, too, had a Jerry Mahoney puppet-doll ... and I have always noticed that Edgar Bergen's actress daughter Candice Bergen speaks out of the side of her mouth, like a ventriloquist, which I assumed she picked up from her father when she was a little girl.

I remember the backs of comic books, when we were young, advertising "THROW YOUR VOICE!" Did ventriloquists ever really throw their voices? The cartoons in the comics showed a voice actually coming from a different part of the room, shocking and delighting young skeptics. Later, the biggest-pulling magazine ad in 1940s and 1950s advertising history had a headline that read, "They laughed when I sat down at the piano...." and it shows a party of people about to be shocked and delighted by a guy who took the ad's piano lessons.

All our lives we have been trying to impress these people in these ads. What more can we do? Write the great American novel? Well, they won't be laughing after THAT!

Maybe writing a novel is a way, if you're good, of throwing your voice. Paul Winchell is dead. Who's got the rights to Mahoney?

Steve

♰   ♰   ♰

4 July 2005 – Los Angeles

Steve.

Have you ever given any thought to becoming a Civil War re-enactor? No? Good. I personally don't get the whole concept. But if you did have Civil War re-enacting on your agenda, I guess I'd have to re-evaluate my whole position on this.

I can completely understand being a Civil War historian. Or simply having an interest in the Civil War. But I have the sneaking suspicion that the serious re-enactor is an addle-brained nerd. You know full well that I have never been a fan of camping out anyway, but to do it with a bunch of other addle-brained nerds while wearing silly costumes strikes me as truly something I would only do under the threat of physical torture.

And yet, thousands of people all over America have specially-made, "authentic" uniforms hanging in their closets, just waiting for the next re-enactment of Bull Run or Antietam. Now I know the great bulk of these closeted blue and gray uniforms are in the South and that certainly explains some of it, but it can't explain it all.

(I have a friend who moved from New York to Athens, Georgia, to take a teaching position at the University of Georgia. She wrote me after she'd been down there a while that she had a very hard time convincing Southerners that in New York whole weeks would go by, sometimes two or three in a row, during which one wouldn't think about the Civil War at all. It's an illness down there.)

Today, however, comes a new argument for not re-enacting: Brian Pohanka, described as "an enthusiastic, well-costumed re-enactor," dead at only 50. Perhaps it's an isolated instance of a Civil War re-enactor not serving his full term, but why take a chance.

An interesting thing in the obit was the mention of Pohanka's being hired by the director of the film *Cold Mountain* to train 5000 Romanian soldiers (using original Civil War drill manuals) to be extras in the film. I keep forgetting, which side did the Romanians fight on in the Civil War?

Pohanka married a fellow re-enactor, who apparently was a real head-turner in her circa-1860s muslin dress. Her name is Marylynne, but she's known as "Cricket." Cricket? Seems a bit much doesn't it?

terry.

5 July 2005
gilbert

terry

Many years ago, before we were married, Kathy and I saw some Civil War theme weddings on TV. It made us think about having our own wedding be a theme wedding, but we never got around to planning it. I first thought about having it be a Knights of the Round Table theme wedding, where she would be Guinevere and I'd be Lancelot. Then years went by and I realized that, given my age I'd have to be King Arthur. Telling this story to Kathy's brother-in-law Bill Olsen one night at dinner he said to me, "Wait much longer to marry her and you can be Merlin!"

Steve

10 july 2005 – Los Angeles

steve.

Out here for Eunice's wedding (un-themed), but of course, still pick up the *NYTimes* for the obits. I was surprised to see one today for a French Nobel Prize in Literature winner. What surprised me was not that he died. Nobel prize winners are allowed to die like the rest of us, I suppose. (Witness Saul Bellow earlier this year.) Rather the surprise was that I had never heard of him. This isn't some Angolan experimental poet. This is a French novelist and I've never heard of him!

Claude Simon, 91 – ever heard of him? – took home the hardware from Sweden in 1985. He wrote twelve novels, with *The Flanders Road* being considered his masterpiece.

Here's what the critics had to say about him: "Many readers found him challenging because he often ignored literary conventions like narrative, structure or plot. His books sought not so much to tell a story but to weave webs of words and associations that had no apparent relationship."

Suddenly I am not so surprised that I'd never heard of this guy.

t.

17 July 2005
gilbert az

dear t

I was sad to see that Christopher Fry died the other day. I didn't know his plays but enjoyed his spirited and unabashedly spiritual poetry. He was 97! Christopher Fry once said, and I have always loved it that he actually said this: "Poetry is the language in which man explores his own amazement ... says heaven and earth in one word ... speaks of himself and his predicament as though for the first time. It has the virtue of being able to say twice as much as prose in half the time, and the drawback, if you do not give it your full attention, of seeming to say half as much in twice the time." That Fry quote always reminds me of my college English professor who in an office visit with me to explore my volatile test scores learned that I was working nights at a factory. She said, "Oh, no, that won't do. You can't read poetry if you are tired."

steve.

July 17, 2005 – New York

Steve,

A trivia question for you, Steve: In what song do the words "the closer and closer I get to home / the more excited I am" appear? So certain am I that you'll get the correct answer, I won't even give you the clue of the singer.

The reason this comes up is that I was singing this song, primarily for the sentiment in those lines, as I was landing at the Detroit airport on June 30th. Okay, so I wasn't singing it out loud – but the song was definitely running through my head.

Miranda had gone directly to Los Angeles for the big run-up to her sister's wedding while I was making the trip in two hops, short-stopping in Detroit for four days along the way. It was a chance to see Lincoln, Allison and my two grandsons.

I must say that though I've lived all over the world and haven't lived in the Midwest in 33 years, I never feel more like I'm coming "home" than when I'm flying into some Midwestern city. I look out the airplane window and see all that familiar flat, flat country, overlaid with the Homestead Act grid still dominantly visible in the rural areas. When I'm landing, even if it's Chicago or Cleveland, I always feel as if I'm "home."

This is, of course, ridiculous. I would never countenance moving back. And as I said, Detroit hasn't actually been my home in more than three decades. Still, as the Neil Young song says, "All my changes were there." Then again, I'm not even sure that's true. Because while many of the most important and formative events of my life did take place while I was in the Midwest, certainly a big chunk of my "changes" took place in other places – Toronto and New York, for instance.

So none of this feeling of "home" is really rationally explainable – and yet it is undeniable. This is what I was feeling while I was back in Michigan for those four days. In the mornings I would get up and drive to our old Adams School neighborhood to do my 35-minute exercise walk there. I'd go to our old house and park across the street in front of Jon Bowers's old house. Then I would basically walk my old paper route: Buckingham, Dorchester, Yorkshire and Maple. I drowned myself in personal nostalgia.

Today I received an e-mail which brought all this, which happened two weeks ago, to mind again. Jon Bowers wrote me with a line saying, "What could be worse than turning 60? How about turning 60 and finding out you have cancer?" He said he was operated on after it was diagnosed and they removed a kidney, but also discovered the cancer had spread to his liver. He is currently recovering his strength enough to start chemotherapy. As you know, I'm hardly an expert on healthcare issues, but none of that sounds very good to me.

Here we've been writing about death for seven months now and none of it has really hit me that hard. It's as if death has become an abstract concept for me. I've been treating it all very intellectually and even humorously; but now this news and I am reminded of death's power and impact again. I had come to think of the deaths we write about as simply milestones in the pageant of our times, but when Jon writes me, I am suddenly hit by the particularity and finality of it all.

(I also find, as I read this over, that I become shockingly inarticulate in trying to express my feelings on this. Death now feels like a totally different subject than what we've been writing about before.)

Jon, by the way, seems in fine spirits and about as positive as a man can be under the circumstances. And finally: the song is "Smokey Mountain Boy," one of Elvis's lesser known songs – but a good one I've always thought – from the movie *Kissin' Cousins*.

t.

July 18, 2005, Gilbert:

Terry,

About the song. When you asked if I knew it from the lyric. My first thought was it was a King Crimson (1960s acid rock band) song, or, no, it's Grand Funk Railroad with their lyric "I'm getting closer to my home" from their song "I'm Your Captain." Or maybe this, finally, is the acid flashback I was promised in the 60s?

Thanks for the news about Jon Bowers and his cancer. I remember, when we were younger, playing ball in the empty lot near Bowers' house, we thought 60 was the ultimate in old age. It was a symbol of being really old.

Today, things are different. Today, health rules, for the most part. One of my heroes is Paul Bragg, who pioneered the health food movement in the United States and inspired Jack LaLanne. Bragg lived to be 95, dying from a surfboarding accident while frolicking like a 20-year-old in rough ocean waters. He claimed we could all live to 120 if we exercised and ate right, and it looked like he was headed there despite having been a very sick child. (He prayed that if they could cure him he would devote his life to health. They did...and he did.) Today many people who are way past 60 but don't look it—people like Clint Eastwood—attribute their eating and exercise programs to Paul Bragg.

Pictures of Bragg in his books when he was 90 look like he's the "60" we thought of. Kathy refers to "the old 60" (really old-looking and old-acting 60-year-olds) and "the new 60" which is hopefully you and me and a fully recovered Jon Bowers.

Although I grew up in Michigan, I moved to Arizona after high school and have pretty much remained here. (I've lived briefly, since then, in California, Germany, North Carolina, and northern Michigan, but Arizona is my home.) I love it that you cited Neil Young's lyric, "All my changes were there." Young's most recent album, "Prairie Wind," is a good album and many say it's as good as it is because he was facing death when he wrote it. He had a serious brain disorder and didn't know if he would survive so he went to Nashville to record his last album, in case he didn't.

This calls to mind the Samurai concept of "Dying before you go into battle" so you will battle with full and fearless abandon. Or like in the Kevin Costner baseball movie, *For Love of the Game*, wherein his Detroit Tigers pitcher character learns again to pitch well by learning to "clear the mechanism" on the mound before pitching. In other words, to go to the state that the Samurai warriors call "no mind."

Alan Watts said we should not fear death because we were there before we were born and it caused us no problem back then. I sent you the Watts book on this subject when your father died, called *The Wisdom of Insecurity*. To Watts, death is a part of life, the tails to the heads of life on an ever-tossing coin.

All my changes occurred for me after I suffered the living death of active alcoholism. Alcoholism is a form of ongoing and relative (but not absolute) suicide. After that recovery, through the 12-Step method, I encountered other expanding levels of recovery and indeed even personal and accelerated evolution toward the spirit that knows no death. And I've devoted my life to helping others do the same. All my books and all my seminars and consulting are part of showing others what has happened for me.

Oh, you might say that *Two Guys Read Moby-Dick* is a departure from that personal growth path, but not totally! In fact, it was an expression of my desire to have fun doing what I love to do.

And inside the fun of the *Moby-Dick* book you and I wrote, is a glimmer of that evolution. We, after all, were pioneers. Tony Robbins should be envious. All those phony self-help gurus who tell you to do things they themselves have never done should be envious, because we actually did it! We pioneered, because we realized the truth that no one, not one person, had ever read *Moby-Dick*. We would be the first and we would report back to the world WHAT IT WAS LIKE to have to read that book, every word, cover to cover. Oh, yes, many people have read parts of the book. And many have read Cliff's Notes. Many have studied that book, and quoted from it, and written about it. But until we did it, no one had ever really read it.

"I read it!" said Thom Beers at the wedding you and I attended in Laurel Canyon or some such place in California. Beers, a reality-TV docudrama producer, had just asked me what kind of books I wrote and I said that I'd just written one with you called *Two Guys Read Moby-Dick*. I told him the premise of the book, and he said, "*Moby-Dick?* I read it!" I was suspicious of this claim, so I asked him.

"Every page? Every word? Cover to cover?"

"Well, maybe not," he said. "No, of course not. Not every page. But I basically read it."

"Well, you didn't read it," I said. "Just admit that you haven't read it, not all of it, and that nobody has. Until now!"

And maybe someone will write a review of this book here, this book about obituaries, and the review will say, "No one's really looked at death before! Or the meaning of life. At least, not through the prism of *Kissin' Cousins*. Not until now."

s.

((our biographers will fastidiously note that the wedding referred to actually took place in November, not July....but our dear reader will never know or care))

[Note: I wanted to write about my visit to Detroit and Jon Bowers' cancer for some time, but simply didn't know how to do it. So I never got around to doing so until November. At which time I back-dated the e-mail so that it fit basically within the proper time frame. On November 5th, Steve and I both attended the wedding of my nephew Nick in Los Angeles and sat at a table with the Thom Beers Steve mentions in his response to my e-mail. Of course it would make no sense for Steve to suddenly be responding to an e-mail I wrote months before, so Steve also back-dated his response.

Is this clarifying anything? Basically its all my fault for being so tardy in writing Steve about the Detroit trip and Jon. And then it's no doubt further my fault for trying to explain it all. Steve's right; you readers don't really care. But I do want to set the record straight for our biographers. tnh.]

20 July 2005

Steve.

General Westmoreland died on Monday night somewhere in his home state of South Carolina and yesterday (Tuesday) he made the front page of the *NYTimes*. The obit seemed fairly (meaning "suitably") long and complete. The overall tone was that the man had made a monumental error in judgment that cost thousands of lives and much national angst and embarrassment.

When Westmoreland went to Viet Nam, there were 15,000 U.S. troops "in country." When he was finally relieved of his post there and kicked upstairs, there were 500,000 U.S. soldiers in Viet Nam and he wanted another 250,000 or so more plus approval to extend the war into Laos, Cambodia and North Viet Nam. A military historian is quoted as saying Westmoreland suffered from "self-delusion." It went on to say that he later failed as a politician (in a losing bid for governor in South Carolina) and as a litigant (when he had to drop his $120-million lawsuit against CBS, who had basically said he wasn't a very good general).

All of this seemed a reasonably fair assessment to me, or at least a logical and defensible one. Which is why I was so surprised when today, Wednesday the 20th, a *new* Westmoreland obituary appeared. I mean what was wrong with the old one?

For the most part, this second obit, written by two writers, Eric Page and Craig R. Whitney (while the first was written only by Page), seemed to give the general much more of the benefit of the doubt. Personally I have no way of knowing whether he was a good general or a bad general, whether he was smart or dumb (though his home state would seem to argue for the latter), so I don't really care about the assessment part.

What does interest me is the two obits. Maybe you can help. After all, you worked at a newspaper for several years. You know that obits of famous and getting-on-in-years figures are written in advance of their deaths. They're then kept on file and pulled out when the subject walks away from the game. All that remains is to fill in the date and circumstances of death and then run the thing. Right?

So why two – rather different – obits on the general? The man died at 91! So it's not as if he caught the *Times* off guard with his death and they scrambled to put together an obit for the Tuesday paper. Was there pressure and backroom politics brought to bear? And if so, to what end? If the point of the second obit was to present a more positive – or at least more balanced – impression of Westmoreland, then in the end, I must say, I think it failed. For though the overall impression might be better, the second obit quotes Westmoreland after Viet Nam as saying, "The record of the American military services of never having lost a war is still in tact." Reading this, our suspicions are confirmed: Westmoreland is from South Carolina.

◦————◦

Frankly, it was obituaries of people like this – men and women closely associated with the seminal events of our times – that attracted me to this project in the first place. These deaths would give two ordinary guys – perhaps somewhat more intelligent and aware than most, but still, just two guys – the chance to write about our impressions of these events.

So here we have a major player in the Viet Nam War die and I don't know what to say. I mean from the ages of twenty to thirty, this war was a major factor in how we lived our lives. Very probably *the* major factor. This, despite the fact that neither one of us ever served in Viet Nam. The fact of the war and the draft affected so many decisions that we made during that time. I probably wouldn't have gone to law school if it hadn't been for Viet Nam; you never would have lived in California or Berlin.

The war affected us in ways that, say, putting a man on the moon or the civil rights movement never did. And yet in the intervening three decades I don't seem to have drawn any coherent conclusions about it. Can this actually be true?

Well, maybe there are *some* things I can say.

First, I don't think we should have been there. I know that this is an original and iconoclastic point of view – but nonetheless I'm going out there on that limb. I think we got sucked into greater and greater involvement by (generally) men like Westmoreland who thought that with just another thousand, or ten thousand, or hundred thousand troops we could wrap this thing up and come home victorious.

Surely *all* of these men were not from South Carolina? Well then how could they have all been so unanimously stupid? I suspect it had a lot to do with *wanting* to believe it as much as rationally coming to their escalation points of view.

Now in the interest of full disclosure, I must say that my current attitudes on this were not the ones I had in the early stages of the war. In the early years of the war I suppose I thought we were doing the stand-up thing by helping out the South Vietnamese, and that our government knew the situation there and must be doing the right thing. I can remember the moment when I simply could no longer buy Johnson's promises that the latest escalation would put us over the top, and that moment wasn't until 1967. But even after that I was hardly out there manning the barricades and chaining myself to the Pentagon doors.

Maybe the most interesting thing about the war is that it forever raised the level of skepticism of the American public about these wars we seem to keep getting ourselves into. Prior to Viet Nam, our wars were pretty generally supported by the American people. Now it's no longer assumed that "our government knows the situation and must be doing the right thing." Now it's always a public issue whether we should be invading countries, because we now *know* that half the time the government doesn't have a clue.

I also have to ask myself, what would have happened if we'd "won" in Viet Nam? I suspect that if we'd won, we would have resumed commercial and diplomatic relations with North Viet Nam by now and that all of Viet Nam would be a big tourist destination. Just the way things are now. I suppose the only real difference would be that Saigon would simply still be called Saigon instead of Ho Chi Minh City. So I suppose that winds up being the real reason we were there – the right to name the city.

terry.

21 july 2005

terry

Good thinking on Westmoreland. I was in the army during Viet Nam but, as you say, did not go there. Mainly by design. I qualified for a four-year foreign language program that ended me up in Berlin and later North Carolina in a psychological warfare unit.

I am still reflecting, too, on what you wrote about Detroit, and going home thinking about that "Smokey Mountain Boy" song from *Kissin' Cousins*, one of Elvis' more entertaining bad movies.

Two days ago Kathy and I watched *8 Mile*, the Eminem rappers movie set in Detroit, near 9 Mile and Mack. Many references to Warren, Michigan, and even Cranbrook, the private boys' school adjacent to the girls school, Kingswood, where your mother taught drama. In the movie, the meanest black thug rapper is OUTED in the film's pivotal moment for having attended Cranbrook, thereby destroying his street cred.

Throughout the movie the rappers talk about living "in the 313" and I finally realized it was the area code for Detroit. It inspired me to change the name of the gang of a character in a novel I'm almost finished writing. I have set the novel in Royal Oak, Michigan, and the character was originally in a gang in Detroit called Satan's Freaks. But I never liked that name. It sounded too much like an Oakland, California, biker gang name. So I changed it to "Lords of the 313."

What's the point of so much Detroit reflection in a book about obituaries? Death. Death is the point of it. Death brings you home. Death, and the prospect of it, and the nearing of it, causes one to walk his old paper route in Birmingham, Michigan, a suburb of Detroit. A suburb of the 313! Retracing steps. A boy's steps. A man retraces them and ponders a life.

S

July 22, 2005 – nyc

steve.

Yes, a man retraces his steps; yes, a man reflects; all in the face of death. My question is: is that a good thing? Shouldn't we be able to wrap all that up and put it in a freezer somewhere? Will the past always haunt us? And take up good "present" time?

And yet, I am addicted to the past, as I suspect all of us are. Why? Do we think it could have been different? Of course we do.

By the way, let me remind you that when we lived in Birmingham, our area code *was* 313. It wasn't until free numbers started getting scarce that they decided to break the Detroit district into several area codes. Chato and Lincoln *[my brother and oldest son. tnh]*, for instance, both have 248 area codes now, whereas both Bloomfield Hills and Lathrup Village would have been 313 when we were in the area.

What did you think of *8 Mile*, by the way? I saw it when it first came out. With Miranda and her sister. And I delighted in telling them afterwards all of the subtleties of Detroit geographies and references. Do you remember that Jon Bowers (as well as Sammy Walker) went to Cranbrook? I actually thought it was a pretty good film.

I will always see a film set in Detroit. Just because of that "home-tug." On the other hand, I warn you not to see *Four Brothers* (which is different than "The Brothers Four," by the way.) Yes, it's set in Detroit, which is why I went to see it in the first place. However, it has nothing to do with the Detroit we know. In fact, most of the film was actually shot in Toronto. (If you want to see a good ghetto film, don't bother with Detroit. Rent *Hustle and Flow*. It stars one of the actors from *Crash*, which I thought was terrific.)

t.

29 july (my birthday) 2005 – new york

s.

Could not let the waning days of July pass without noting three deaths from the last week. Each seemed prototypically of our lifetime. None of these could have been from the generation before us because they all made their names on the basis of television.

First, James Doohan was beamed up to a better place. He played Scotty in the *Star Trek* TV series. An interesting thing in the obit was the fact that Doohan, a Canadian by birth, served in the Canadian Army and caught six bullets in the D-Day invasion, one of which blew off his right middle finger. His ashes are to be shot into space. That's what it said, honest.

Then Danny Simon, Neil Simon's older brother. He got in on the ground floor when television was just taking off, writing for early TV shows like *Milton Berle*, the *Danny Thomas Show* and the Phil Silvers show, *Sergeant Bilko*. He also wrote for Sid Caesar's *Your Show of Shows*. As you know, anyone who ever worked on that show could get work for the next forty years merely by mentioning that he'd been there. Perhaps this is as good a time as any for me to say that I never really liked the show – never thought it was that funny. So shoot me.

And finally Gerry Thomas. He invented the TV dinner just when, as his obit put it, "television was becoming the dominant family pastime."

When you think about it, we have seen the rise and fall of television. We were in on its birth; we watched it grow to its zenith; and now it has already started to fade as the dominant medium with internet starting to seriously steal TV viewing hours. (I'm leaving that split infinitive.)

———

The other personally more noteworthy death was John Herald. Lead singer and driving force behind the Greenbriar Boys. We used to sing "The Banks of the Ohio," "Stewball" and "Amelia Earhart," all of which we learned from him. Even after the Greenbriar Boys broke up, Herald continued his music, forming a series of other bands. I saw him two or three years ago at a Greenbriar Boys reunion at an outdoor folk concert at Lincoln Center. And he used to play with his own band every other week at the Parkside Lounge on Houston Street just a few blocks from us.

The obit suggested he committed suicide at his home near Woodstock, New York. But was not definitive. When I started writing this I googled him and found two tributes to him written by two guys he was involved with musically.

Apparently he did a concert and went back to his home, wrote and mailed some farewell notes and then killed himself. His body was discovered two days later when one of the letters arrived and the guy called the police to get them to go to the house.

Part of the cause of his depression was money worries. It seemed he had almost no money and pretty much lived hand to mouth. Amazing isn't it that a guy who can get a picture and 400 words in his *New York Times* obituary could be that destitute.

t.

30 July 2005

terry

You struck a nerve with me. I agree that the Golden Age of TV, with Milton Berle and Ernie Kovacs and Sid Caesar, was awful. I never liked it. It was very, well....is "stupid" a word you can use in a book?

I would like to add to your obituary for TV an obit for newspapers. We read daily how circulation of all the major daily papers is going down, down, down and so fast! No matter if the city itself has population gains, the circulation is still going down.

Two death signs: I recently walked out in the early morning to get a sports score that I went to bed too early to see on the TV the night before and I found in the paper that there was no score. The teams just played, but there was no score. Why? The paper had to be PRINTED before the score (west coast) was available. I threw the paper across the room. Second death sign: in a fictional work I am finishing writing I have a smart and aware female character wake up in the morning and sit with her coffee in front of her computer screen to get the morning's news. I do not have her opening the morning paper, because it was not my intention to make her character clueless and tuned-out.

I, myself, usually check my internet news sources before turning in at night. Various blogs and news sites catch me up. When I open the morning paper, I see, quite literally, yesterday's news. Often I see things I saw on the internet two days ago on the front page as news. Dead.

Now I know you love the feature sections of the *NYTimes*, etc. And you and I are children of the old school and we grew up back in the day, so newspapers will never be totally removed from our lives. But they are dead.

Good riddance. The internet is a pure joy to surf for news and comment.

s.

Aug 2, 2005 – New York

Steve.

On my deathbed I'll be asking for the day's newspaper. If they still publish one. But I agree with you: newspapers are gone. Or at least they're being forced to take on a new role. For instance, I think of the *Times* as sort of a daily magazine. But yes it always pisses me off when they don't have the late sports scores. The one that establishes the dividing line is that even the latest edition won't have the score of the Monday Night Football game. That game usually ends at fifteen minutes after midnight or so (EST) but it's too late to get in the paper.

Do you think that if the President was assassinated by some madman at 12:30 at night that it would make the morning papers?

t.

5 Aug. 2006

Terry,

I go to the internet late at night and first thing in the morning to get the news. Not that I'm trying to pass myself off as modern or special. It's just more efficient for me. And I also don't like receiving the politically correct news that newspapers deliver. I want it straight.

s.

8 Aug 2005 – nyc

s.

Well, all the obit news today is about Peter Jennings. And, naturally, he's interesting to me being a Canadian by birth (him, not me) and his being a newsman who still actually wrote some of the stuff he read on air. Still, as much of an icon as he was to so many, I can't really say that he was embedded in my life.

The truth is, despite your pronouncement that the newspaper is dead, I tend to get my news from the morning paper (right now the *NYTimes*, but at various times during the year, also the *Miami Herald* [Mexican edition] or the *Toronto Globe and Mail*). There was a generation that seemed to get hooked on getting their news on television – my own parents and both of my wives' parents were a part of that. When the six or eleven o'clock (depending on how old they were at the time) news came on, everything else stopped.

Quite honestly I don't look down on that. It's just a different way of getting the news. I'm fully as obsessive about reading the paper each day as they were about seeing the six o'clock news. The difference is that while they might see Dan Rather or Peter Jennings as a cultural signpost, I might see someone like Maureen Dowd (who I'm sure you hate) in that role.

So here I am defending the fact that I don't see the death of Peter Jennings as a world crisis when clearly it is. But the fact is, I was more interested in the death the day before of Robin Cook.

There's no real reason that you should be aware of him, but during the three years we lived in London, the man seemed to live on the front page of the English papers. He was first off a rather outspoken Foreign Minister in the cocky-with-their-landslide Blair/ "New" Labour administration of 1997 – the year we moved there.

His outspokenness got him a lot of headlines, but then he really went for glory when he up and dumped his wife in favor of his secretary who he'd been having an affair with for some time apparently. The whole thing was rather ugly with his salt-of-the-earth wife bleeding in public while Cook was pictured holding hands with his new chippy.

Frankly the thing that surprised me was that his secretary, Gaynor Regan, would bother having anything to do with him. Cook was consistently ranked in the top five ugliest men in the world list.

He was a Scot and apparently died of a heart attack at 59. Young, but were you aware that the Scots have the highest heart attack death rate of any of the civilized countries? When I used to work on healthcare businesses in England I noticed that all the clinical trials related to cardio therapies or products were carried out in Scotland. I once asked why and people looked at me as if I were an amateur; of course, everyone knew about the Scottish propensity to heart attacks. Okay, now you do, too.

t.

Aug 10 – Gilbert

Terry.

A story in the paper today was *like* an obit. Detroit, which in 1955 was the nation's fifth largest city, recently fell, for the first time in a century, out of the list of the 10 largest, replaced by San Jose. Detroit is America's saddest city: cattle could be grazed in vast swaths of depopulated neighborhoods. Suffering from a vanishing middle class, and vanished fathers of the 70 percent of children born out of wedlock, the city's decline may be irreversible.

I treasure my memories of Detroit. Where do memories go when you die?

steve.

Aug 11, 2005 – NYC

Steve.

Nobody really interesting, but just to carry on with the Sid Caesar thing. Another "Your Show of Shows" writer went down last week. Gary Belkin. But Belkin goes the Reiner/Brooks crowd one better – he claims he wrote all of Cassius Clay's poetry!

"Here I predict Mr. Liston's dismemberment
I'll hit him so hard he'll wonder where October and November went."

Both George Plimpton, who knew and wrote about Ali, and David Remnick, who wrote an Ali biography, publicly questioned how many of Ali's poems Belkin actually wrote. Belkin says "all." But Plimpton said he personally witnessed Ali writing a poem.

This is obviously destined to be one of those Shakespeare/Bacon disputes that will be debated for centuries.

(Perhaps this might be a good time to mention that Cassius Clay later changed his name to Muhammad Ali. A lot of people probably don't know that. Belkin died with the name he was born with.)

terry.

August 12, 2005

t.

Thanks for mentioning Ali! Ali used to go up to Elvis' suite in Vegas and listen to Elvis and his group sing gospel songs until the sun came up. There are pictures of Ali and Elvis together.

Leaving death for a moment, I want to note the anniversary of the birth this week of Percy Mayfield, one of the great songwriters in American blues and soul music.

My favorite performance of a Mayfield song is by Elvis. When Elvis returned to recording in Memphis in the first burst of activity after his 1968 comeback television special, he recorded Mayfield's "Stranger In My Own Hometown." It is a great song, to which Elvis gave a heartfelt, killer performance. (Track it down on any of the Elvis collections of the songs he recorded at the American Sound Studio in Memphis.)

Mayfield died in 1984. The music survives.

s.

13AUG05 – NYC

Steve.

Remember Mose Allison? He is a jazz pianist and as you know, I'm not wild about jazz, but when I was in college I came upon and fell for a song he sang called "The Seventh Son." The vocal style was unique. Or so I thought. Until just now. After your last e-mail I googled Percy Mayfield and was directed to Mose Allison's website. In the bio of Mose it says that his vocal style was patterned on Percy Mayfield's.

t.

14 August 2005\gilbert

dear ter,

Ted Radcliffe died yesterday in Chicago. He was 103. He was one of the last surviving "Negro leagues" baseball stars.

"I've had a good life," Radcliffe told an interviewer shortly before he died. "We couldn't stay in the white hotels then. The only place we stayed in a white hotel was up around North Dakota or Canada. But then, some people never had the opportunity we had. Some people come along and dig ditches all their lives."

Radcliffe was both a pitcher and a catcher. On his catching vest he had painted the words, "Thou Shalt Not Steal."

And although he was, in the 1920s and 1930s, a victim of racism, he did not seize upon that victim status and allow it to define him. He enjoyed his 103 years on this planet. It seems like he insisted on that joy.

There is an email circulating through the internet today recalling the good old days. When self-reliance was admired more than your victim status. Somehow I link Radcliffe to that feeling. The writer of the email is anonymous, but I would like to include it here because it reminds me of you and me growing up together in little Birmingham, Michigan, being just like this guy:

My mom used to cut chicken, chop eggs and spread mayo on the same cutting board with the same knife and no bleach, but we didn't seem to get food poisoning. My mom used to defrost hamburger on the counter AND I used to eat it raw sometimes, too. Our school sandwiches were wrapped in wax paper in a brown paper bag, not in icepack coolers, but I can't remember getting e. coli.

Almost all of us would have rather gone swimming in the lake instead of a pristine pool (talk about boring), no beach closures then.

The term cell phone would have conjured up a phone in a jail cell, and a pager was the school PA system.

We all took gym, not PE ... and risked permanent injury with a pair of high top Keds (only worn in gym) instead of having cross-training athletic shoes with air cushion soles and built in light reflectors. I can't recall any injuries, but they must have happened because they tell us how much safer we are now.

Not a single person I knew had ever been told that they were from a dysfunctional family. How could we possibly have known that? We needed to get into group therapy and anger management classes. We were obviously so duped by so many societal ills, that we didn't even notice that the entire country wasn't taking Prozac! How did we ever survive?

s

12 aug 2005 – NYC

Steve.

I too was struck by the Ted Radcliffe obit in the *Times*. Like you I admired a number of Radcliffe's qualities – not the least of which was his longevity. But I gotta say that it in no way put me in mind of anything resembling the sappy piece by the anonymous e-mail writer you quote.

Steve – get a grip!

That the-old-days-were-better tone of mind is what you've always railed against. The old days were not better. They may have been different. And they were *our* days so the sentimental among us (and that includes me) may look back on them with a certain nostalgia – but they were not better. Death by nostalgia.

Terry.

Gilbert, AZ. – August 14, 2005

Dear TER

Boy, I agree and now regret – but won't withdraw – that sentimental Good Old Days email message ... I do agree with you that times just keep getting better, even though many modern hysterics think otherwise. For a moment, I was one. But you gotta love that email.

Here's another example that makes your point:

LIFE EXPECTANCY (Years)

Cro-Magnon Era	18
Ancient Egypt	25
1400 Europe	30

1800 Europe and USA	37
1900 USA	48
2002 USA	78

You are right that times get better. Even mathematically.

I want to live long because I have not done my work yet. My true work as a writer has not been produced in my own mind. I have approached it. I published my first book when I was 49, so I started "late," (maybe, though that may have been an advantage) but there are certain kinds of books I have not yet written. This being one of them. This being one! Our book about *Moby-Dick* being another. Not to make myself important. Or to leave a legacy. But for the love of it.

You became an award-winning playwright at the age of 61. They say Paul McCartney gave the best live concert of his life here in Phoenix this week. He's 62? What does age really matter anymore? It's how you spend your day. Not your years, but your day. Is my feeling about it.

How do people want to die? I know that this year there was voting on physician-assisted suicide in Oregon. The Bush administration tried to intervene, but if they were true conservatives they would honor states' rights in the matter and let Oregon be Oregon. Kathy and I had a friend who died yesterday at the age of 91 and she had Alzheimer's. Her name was Ardie Frost, and she was a beautiful, creative, energetic, funny woman who will be missed on this poorer-now planet. Wherever she went when she died is where I want to go (and I think your father is there, too.)

Jonathan Franzen wrote an amazing essay on his father's Alzheimer's recently. Saying he was angry that there was some hidden bliss in the disease, being able to smell, with delight, the same rose seven times in one day, as if for the first surprisingly delightful time.

Tom T. Hall started his song "Old Dogs and Children and Watermelon Wine" with the words, "How old do you think I am?" Remember, too, that McCartney wrote "When I'm 64" when he was in his 20s thinking it was an absurd age, a hilariously old age for a Beatle to ever be. Now he's a couple years away.

I asked our friend Fred Knipe how he wanted to die and he said he wanted to be eaten by a large crab. He said he wanted to be strolling along the sea shore one day and he wanted a huge crab to emerge from the ocean and take him on the spot. He wanted to go that way, and wanted everyone to know that that was how he died. We all have our wishes. My kids used to ask me how I wanted to die, and I said I wanted to "die laughing in my sleep." If I do, it may be in a dream where I'm in Connecticut watching a performance of your play, *Hamlet - The Sequel.* Maybe the curtain has yet to rise, and I'm in my seat looking at the program, where it lists the cast and says, "Tom Cruise: As himself." I laugh. The end.

Steve.

13aug2005.

Steve.

The joy of Alzheimer's: You're constantly meeting new people.

t.

18 august 2005
Gilbert

Ter.

THANKS for the photo of you and Miranda ... in Mexico??? *[In fact, the picture was taken in July in the Hamptons on the back porch of the home of friends we were visiting for the weekend. tnh]* You looking great with white hair!!!!! And a bright red shirt!!! Collar up like a cool guy!!!! Old, but ALIVE! And writing – and ready for 30 more years of productivity. I submit the words of William Butler Yeats now:

When you are old and grey and full of sleep,
And nodding by the fire, take down this book,

And slowly read, and dream of the soft look
Your eyes had once, and of their shadows deep;
How many loved your moments of glad grace,
And loved your beauty with love false or true,
But one man loved the pilgrim Soul in you,
And loved the sorrows of your changing face;
And bending down beside the glowing bars,
Murmur, a little sadly, how Love fled
And paced upon the mountains overhead
And hid his face amid a crowd of stars.

s.

Aug 20, 2005

steve.

You know I've always been a Yeats fan and the poem you cite was one of my favorites. But let me ask you something, was the poem quoted in the movie *Peggy Sue Got Married*? Yes, I know, it seems unlikely, but this notion keeps sticking in my mind.

Still, what I really wanted to write you about was the disturbing news that a second young member of Tony Blair's initial 1997 cabinet died. Like Robin Cook, whose death I noted less than two weeks ago, Mo Mowlam was also outspoken and a media sound-bite favorite.

In 1997 she was diagnosed with a brain tumor. Between then and now she was going through radiotherapy, which at times made her unsteady on her feet. Two weeks ago she fell and hit her head. She went into a coma and died yesterday. She was only 55.

I must say it was a fun time to be living in Britain – 1997-99. The Blair government swept into power with a huge majority and there was a great sense of hope for the future. Sort of what we felt in the US when Kennedy came in. Of course now Blair's government has lost a great deal of its support. It's been hit by a few financial scandals; and, in a hugely unpopular move in the UK, Blair sided with the US in invading Iraq, earning him the reputation as a Bush toady. In fact, Robin Cook, who was Foreign Secretary at the time of the invasion, resigned from the cabinet in protest and was replaced by Jack Straw, who is a *Blair* toady. I suppose great promise is always fated to disappoint.

    And now two Blair cabinet ministers, both in their 50s, die within a couple of weeks of each other. Do these things happen in threes?

t.

Aug 27 – gilbert

Terry.

    This for the front or back or middle of 2GRTO:

    To avoid the clichés
    Of the obituary writers,
    Die in obscurity.
    A fine bed in a light-filled room
    Someone who adores you is at your side
    And vowed to silence.

        Kenneth Koch, "Aesthetics of Obituary"

Or … as Bonnie Raitt says:

    Life
    is
    more
    precious
    when
    there's

less
of
it
to
live

steve.

Aug 29, 2005 – saratoga springs, NY

steve

Or how about TS Eliot:

"Our life is unwelcome, our death
  Unmentioned in the *Times*."

t.

3 sept 2005 (Labour Day weekend) – Georgian Bay, Ontario, Canada

Steve.

Just in case there's any doubt about the country I'm in, just look at my spelling of Labour Day. We're here on Georgian Bay for five weeks and I'm wondering what it'll be like getting my obits from a different paper over this time.

We're kind of out in the woods. I wouldn't say it was really out in the middle of nowhere because we're only a couple of hours north of Toronto; still, it's tough to get *The New York Times* here. It arrives (when it arrives) a day late, and it involves about a 25-mile drive and often ends with the woman at the newsstand saying: "Nope, it didn't come in today." So I'll be getting my obits from the *Toronto Star* or the *Toronto Globe and Mail* over the next little while. Both are pretty good papers, actually, and I can pick either up in Lafontaine which is only about 3 miles away.

Over the years I have found I have something of a facility for getting into local things quickly. When we were living in London I became a fan of English football and followed British politics. In Paris, we grew to understand the ins and outs of their baffling political system and also got hooked on PSG (the Paris football team: Paris-St. Germain) and steeplechase racing at d'Auteuil. And in a brief two months in Barcelona I became sort of a Catalonian Nationalist. I suppose I do this because, as much as I love to travel, I hate being seen as a tourist. I want to live in the community rather than just tour the sights. I know this is foolish. Obviously I stick out like a sore thumb as an American with but a tenuous grasp of the native language. Still, I enjoy making the effort. All of this starts with reading the local papers. So the *Globe* and the *Star* it will be.

But my obit reading up here started even before I picked up my first Toronto paper. As every year, we're staying at the beautiful cottage of friends of ours (Rod and Nancy Skelton) and when we arrived, Nancy gave me a packet of some Toronto newspaper clippings that she had been intending to give to me for some time. Just how long a time became clear when I noticed that two of the items were an obit and an "appreciation" from March 6th ... of 2004! She had waited more than a year to get them to me.

I was glad she'd gotten them to me in the end however, for they were the death notices of my former accountant. The actual obit from the *Globe* had been written by a writer who used to work for me when I was working in advertising in Toronto in the early '70s.

So how does an accountant (my accountant!) get more than 1000 words in the *Globe and Mail* on his death? I'm not sure really.

I always liked him. And he was, to the extent I am qualified to make this judgment, a "good" accountant. But still, can you think of any other accountant anywhere who gets even a mention in the obituary section when he dies? Much less over a thousand words?

Arthur – that was his name, Arthur Gelgoot – did it by making himself the accountant to the artistic community in Toronto.

The headline in the *Globe* obit: "He was an exciting accountant."

The obit played off the stereotype of creative people as total nitwits with money and showed Arthur as the magician who put their financial lives in order. His list of clients included a few hundred of the top names in the Toronto art, stage, film, music, media, dance and literary scenes. And me.

I knew he had died (Nancy had told me when it happened). But I hadn't seen the obituaries until today. They quite amazed me.

t.

5 sept. 2005 – gilbert

Ter.

One thing I don't like about this book so far is my habit of merely observing various particular deaths, without solving death itself. Yet. As an issue. Maybe I've been too busy to do that.

My work keeps me busy. I am very busy, and my work is good, and fulfilling, and now I even have appeared on TV for a day, so I can TIVO or tape it when it appears in October for people to watch after I myself am dead so I won't seem so dead...just like Elvis HARDLY hardly hardly seems dead when you hear "Hound Dog" cranked way up on the car radio...how can THAT sound be dead? Anyway, all this leads to a quote from the great John Updike who said, quite relevant to this thinking here:

> "For many men, work is the effective religion, a ritual occupation and inflexible orientation which permits them to imagine that the problem of their personal death has been solved."

S

21SEPT2005 – Georgian Bay, Ontario, Canada

steve.

You no doubt saw Simon Wiesenthal's obituary today. 96 he was! I don't know what paper you're reading, but I'm sure it was a substantial obit. The *Toronto Globe and Mail* had a full page on him – well deserved I'm sure. Certainly a key figure in what must be the most clearly black-and-white issue of the last century – the Holocaust.

Still, I found myself much more taken with an obituary the *G&M* ran yesterday on Eddy Tomera. You've never heard of him. Neither had I until I read his obit – and maybe that's why I was so caught up in it.

Tomera was born in Poland in 1928. At the age of 13 he was taken from his family farm by the conquering Germans and put into a slave labor camp south of Hamburg. He emigrated to Canada at 22, worked in gold mines in Quebec, married, became a farmer and later a farm manager for various city-slickers from Montreal who bought "gentleman farms" but needed someone with some farming experience to run them. He died at 76.

So why'd Eddy get this rather long notice in Canada's leading paper? I think it might have had something to do with the fact that he hung out at a bar near Masonville, Quebec, called the Owl's Nest. He used to have a few drinks and play pool there with, among others, Mordecai Richler. Richler, who died a couple of years ago, was one of Canada's leading writers and novelists. In his last novel – *Barney's Version* – which I just read (and loved) last month, he immortalized the Owl's Nest by making it one of the hero's hangouts. If he hadn't done so, I doubt I would ever have had the chance to read about Eddy Tomera's interesting life. And a life very much affected, you might even say *shaped*, by the events of the times.

You may remember that Richler, who was a baseball fan and would occasionally write about the game, wrote a glowing blurb for Dad's book – *I Don't Care If I Never Come Back*. Dad loved Richler as a novelist and was thrilled with the blurb. In fact after Dad's death, I found in his papers a letter to Richler thanking him for his kind words on his book. It appeared that the letter had never been mailed, so I sent it on to Richler saying I thought he'd appreciate it even though it was nine years late and I explained how I'd come across it. He wrote me back thanking me for sending it on and mentioned that if I was ever in Montreal to give him a call and we'd meet somewhere for a drink.

Well, of course, I never did. But now, I wish to hell I had. It would have been worth a special trip.

t.

Sept 23 – gilbert

Ter.

I think your father's book on baseball is the best book ever written about baseball. Thanks for reminding me of it.

And speaking of baseball, somehow I missed this at the time, but Frank "Pig" House, who played in the major leagues for 10 seasons, died on March 13, 2005 in Birmingham, Ala. He was 75.

House hit .248 in his career with 47 home runs and 235 RBI. The catcher played for Detroit, Kansas City and Cincinnati. His most productive season came in 1955 when he hit .259 for the Tigers with 15 home runs and 53 RBI.

According to his obituary, House signed with the Tigers in 1948 for $75,000 and two automobiles. He was 20 years old when he made his debut with the team in 1950.

In November 1957, the Tigers traded House, Kent Hadley, Duke Maas, Jim Small, John Tsitouris, Bill Tuttle and Jim McManus to Kansas City for Gus Zernial, Billy Martin, Tom Morgan, Lou Skizas, Mickey McDermott and Tim Thompson. A lot of names in that trade and they bring back a lot of memories.

House later was elected to the Alabama Legislature and, his obituary states, led the effort to create the Alabama Sports Hall of Fame in 1967. He became a member of that Hall of Fame in 1975. In 2004, the Frank "Pig" House Award was announced to recognize contributors to Alabama sports. All of this info from the Associated Press obituary.

And did you remember him being called "Pig"?

I hope it was dropped after baseball or maybe I don't hope that; maybe I hope the continuance of that nickname made death rest easier on him.

s.

24SEPT2005 – Georgian Bay, Ontario, Canada

s.

I do actually recall his nickname was Pig. Not that I'd ever have called him that to his face. But if you'd asked me a week ago what Frank House's nickname was, I'd have said Pig without flinching. I will also say that there are 13 names mentioned in that KC-Detroit trade and not one of them is in the Hall of Fame (unless you count the Alabama Sports Hall of Fame), but to my credit (?) I can honestly say that I remember 11 of those players. The only ones I don't recall are Jim McManus and Tim Thompson.

I'm going to forgive myself on those two. I just looked them up. McManus played a grand total of 5 games in the Bigs; Thompson played in 187, but only 4 with Detroit.

After our last year's correspondence became a book (*Two Guys Read Moby-Dick*), it would probably be a bit disingenuous of us to play like we don't know we're trying to write a book here. So I think it's fair to raise this question: can you come up with the names of three people anywhere in the world who would be interested in anything in these last two letters? I know I can come up with two pretty quickly, but then I'm stumped for a third.

t.

Sept 27, 2005 – PHX-AZ

Terry,

Let's just write what we want! Who cares if people skip a few paragraphs?

Lawrence Block wrote a long intro to a book written by Dave Van Ronk, a kind of Village folk memoir about the days when people were authentic (genuine fakes) and Dylan was trying to write like Eliot (TS) and sing like Elliot (Ramblin' Jack), and it turns out that Block himself has confused a world-weary bitterness about the profession of writing with personal street cred parallel to that of Van Ronk when truth has it that he has as much street cred as Kanye West the fresh prince of fake rap, the ABBA of modern hip hop.

Kathy and I spent a day at a workshop in Prescott to learn from Lawrence Block about how to write. Interesting experience. But terrible. If he dies this year I'll recount that experience in these letters. He better hang on to his life. It's up to him.

s.

1 October 2005 – Gilbert

dear t,

M. Scott Peck, the author of *The Road Less Traveled*, died this week at the age of 69. Pancreatic and liver duct cancer. Any relation to the drinking he was trying to cut back on? We may never know.

What I do know is that his great book was one of the true inspirations in my life. I sometimes think *The Road Less Traveled* was where the phrase "a life-changing book" first came from. It was a book that had the power to give the reader hope and love and light. I know the book felt like it had restored power in me. Power that had leaked out through adult life. This very personal book tore the mask off the psychotic fear we have in adult life of the false power of circumstance and other people.

Peck's book demonstrated through the grace of his brilliantly clear writing that true power is in the mind and spirit. (And he made no distinction between them!) Peck showed how spirit appears not through grace or luck or joining the right religion but through self-discipline. Taking charge of the self!

A respected and successful friend recently told me that my most recent book was, for him, the best book since *The Road Less Traveled*. He was delusional. But, still, he knew which book to compare mine to to give me the greatest compliment.

s.

7 October – Georgian Bay, Ontario, Canada

s.

Just a few weeks ago I read that the playwright August Wilson had some terminal illness and was on deathwatch. The watch is over: he died a few days ago. Liver cancer. The man was a year younger than I am. But what he accomplished!

Just this year he completed his Pittsburgh Hill District Cycle of ten plays, one for each decade of the last century. The last one, *Radio Golf*, will come to Broadway in the next few months after tryout runs in New Haven and Los Angeles.

I feel, having lived mainly in New York since 1985, that I should have seen more of his plays in person. To be honest, I'm not quite sure why I didn't. The only one I ever saw was *Jitney*. And I saw that on the London stage when we were living there. I loved it. And now, of course, I wish I'd seen all the others, particularly *Fences* and *Ma Rainey*. I suspect I'll get the chance over the next few years, assuming I'm around, because I'm sure they'll all be done again.

t.

10 Oct. 2005

dear t

Your writing about the death of playwright August Wilson reminds me that your own play – *Hamlet - The Sequel* – is having a staged reading later this month somewhere in New England. I must say that when it won the Playhouse on the Green playwriting competition and was honored appropriately, I was happy about it for two reasons:

1) It's a delightful comedy, thereby bringing joy and laughter to intelligent theater-goers and play-readers (versus August Wilson's anger and anguish).

And 2), I praised the play lavishly when I read it, ranking it up there with my favorite Woody Allen plays (which I used to go see when they all starred Tony Roberts) and received a wary, uncertain response from you to my praise. Wondering if I was being authentic, or just trying to encourage a friend to keep writing. I am vindicated! I was right. Others can see its merit, too. Listen to me. I know. Hooray. Now tell me what it was like to go to the reading!

s.

11 OCT 2005 – Toronto, Canada (on the way back to NYC)

Steve.

The "professional reading" of my play is part of the prize. It hasn't happened yet – scheduled for the 26th. I am frankly a bit nervous. I mean, you've read the play, it's about kids in their mid-twenties in the East Village of New York. When I had lunch with the director in June she asked me about my casting thoughts. Specifically she asked me what age I saw my characters.

"About 27," I said, just pulling a specific age out of a hat.

"That's exactly the age I was thinking," she said.

And yet, while I was in Georgian Bay I talked to her on the phone and she told me she'd found some actors she thought would be good and wondered out loud if I might be willing to expand the age range of the players up to the mid-to-late forties! I had visions of her conducting auditions in the Bridgeport Senior Citizens home.

"I don't know," I dissembled.

"Well, I'll keep looking," she said.

You will understand my fears.

We'll see. I wish I were there, working with her now. But the fact is I will show up in the morning of the day of the show (the 26th) and see the final run-throughs. By then the die (or the play) will be cast. I really have no say at that point. I'll let you know how it goes. What would August Wilson have done?

t.

13 Oct. 2005
Gilbert

Ter,

Hey, today, 40 is young! Let them be in their forties. They will be better actors. Wish I could go.

Steve

16 OCT 2005 –New York, NY

Steve.

I can clearly remember where I was – in fact the exact room I was in – when I heard on the radio the news that the last Civil War veteran had died. Knowing the house I was in lets me place the date as 1953 or '54. The Civil War ended in April of 1865 so it had been

88 or 89 years since this vet had seen service. The radio report said this guy had joined the Confederate Army as a drummer boy at the age of 14 and had served for several years so obviously at death he was a few years over the century mark.

At the time, hearing this news made the Civil War seem almost a contemporary event. All this came back to me as I read in the *New York Times* about the death of William Allan, 106, the last surviving Australian to have served in combat in World War I. The reason for the "to have served in combat" language is that there is another Australian WWI vet still hanging on, but he was a radio operator and was never posted to a combat zone.

Three thoughts:

1) Has some current ten-year-old just heard about Allan and now thinks of WWI, for the first time, as an almost contemporary event? It has, after all, only been 86 years since the Armistice.

2) I'm pulling for you to live to be the last surviving Viet Nam vet, although never posted to a combat zone. Which seems to me, by the way, as much the best way to serve in a war. I'm also planning on being around myself to see you achieve this honor. And ...

3) Do you think there are any surviving American WWI vets? And why didn't the *NYTimes* obit tell us this?

t.

19 Oct. 2005
Gilbert

terry

True I served four years in the army during the Viet Nam era, but I am not a Viet Nam vet. According to official army documents that I received when I took advantage of the G.I. Bill to go back to college I was officially listed as a "COLD WAR VETERAN."

I once pointed that out to your father, who served in WWII, and he laughed for a long time. But I served in a frigid Berlin, where the Wall was all around us. And my job, as a Russian linguist, was to keep electronic tabs on the Russians in East Berlin, their telephone systems being so technologically crude and insecure that people like me could listen in, tape them, and transcribe the salient bits of intelligence to pass along to Washington, DC.

S

20-OCT-2005 – NY

Steve,

Okay then I guess I'll have to root for you to be the last surviving Cold War vet.

t.

23 oct – PHX, AZ

Ter.

Two weekends ago I became a real Northwestern fan....today I watched them totally clobber MSU. They are a fun team.

Odd *NYT* obit today … a woman mentioned in this obit had become a friend of mine in Tucson – Ann Risley – I introduced her to Fred who went out with her a number of times.

> BOSTON, Oct. 19 (Reuters) – The actor Charles Rocket, whose unscripted profanity on "Saturday Night Live" in 1981 cost him his network television job, was found dead near his Connecticut home on Oct. 7. He was 56.
>
> He committed suicide by cutting his throat, Sgt. J. Paul Vance of the Connecticut State Police said.

The actor, whose real name was Charles Claverie, was a cast member of the NBC show "Saturday Night Live" in the 1980-81 season. During a parody of the "Who Shot J. R.?" episode of "Dallas," his character was shot, and Mr. Rocket uttered the obscenity while saying he would like to know who did it. After viewers complained, NBC apologized. Mr. Rocket; two fellow cast members, Gilbert Gottfried and Ann Risley; and four of the show's writers were dismissed.

Mr. Rocket's movie credits included "Earth Girls Are Easy," "How I Got Into College," "Dumb and Dumber" and "Dances With Wolves." He also had roles in the 1980's television series "Moonlighting" and "Max Headroom," and provided voices for several cartoon characters.

Mr. Rocket is survived by his wife, Beth, and son, Zane.

Steve.

24 OCT 2005 – New York, NY

Steve.

Wow! I can see you being stopped by the incidental mention of someone you know in an obit. Worse, of course, if she had been the *subject* of the obit.

But a few other things struck me about the notice:

1) If you were going to commit suicide and were evaluating the various executional options, where on the list would cutting your own throat be? It would be very low on my list.

2) I worked on a series of commercials with the director of the feature film *Max Headroom* (a movie, I must admit, I've never seen). Farhad Mann was his name, though I'm not

100% certain of the spelling. This is an item in the "it's a small world" category. And finally …

3) How would you like to wander about the (small) world with the name Zane Rocket? The best thing that can be said, I guess, is that at least people would remember your name at cocktail parties. I would at any rate.

The director of my play told me she'd found and cast more appropriately aged actors. She sent me the names of the two leads and I googled them. Pleased to report that neither of them looked as if they were eligible for Social Security.

t.

26 October 2005
gilbert

dear terry

Rosa Parks died this week, and I have always loved her, not only for the courageous stand she took, refusing to give up her seat to a white man, and thereby inspiring Martin Luther King to create the whole civil rights movement, but for more than that.

I loved her because she took a stand against human anger. I heard a tape of a talk she gave in the late 1990s and when a media person asked her if she wasn't still angry that she would have to even go through a civil rights movement, she said no. She said she wasn't even angry when they arrested her for not surrendering her seat. She said anger wasn't useful to her. It didn't serve her, or the movement.

The media person was very disappointed. The media person was hoping for rage, for stories of how Rosa might have cried softly into her pillow each night. But no. She GOT MORE DONE in an upbeat, proactive frame of mind. She was a literal victim of racism but she refused to PLAY victim.

Most angry people waste their whole lives playing victim. Blaming people who have done them wrong. An ex-husband, a jerk of a boss. And as Rosa Parks so wisely realized, these are ineffective people. Just as Malcolm X was less effective in his brilliant fury than Martin Luther King in his less brilliant decision to focus on the dream he had. Less brilliant, but wiser and more effective.

I think Rosa Parks is a great American. In my seminars I almost always use her as an example of someone it would be great to be. She was courageous, she was effective and she was happy. She was the light.

S.

26 October 2005 – NYC

Steve.

You kind of threw me with your Rosa Parks note. After all, you talked to me on the phone just yesterday saying (in your deadpan facetious way) you were going to come down hard on the woman, rake her over the coals. You were going to suggest that she should *not* have taken that seat on the bus – should have given it up to a white man, depending, of course, on exactly how white he was.

Instead, you reported in with this glowing eulogy for the lady and said you always point her up in your seminars as a life-model for all human beings. You sly dog. I guess your inner-Democrat got the better of you. Well, I'm glad, because as lively and fun as it would have been to take that contrarian position I think it would have been wrong.

In a law school course I took – called "The Philosophy of Law" – we discussed this very issue. Well, not Rosa Parks *per se*, but the issue of civil disobedience.

It was the contention of our professor that a man could believe in the rule of, and necessity for, man-made law and yet still believe in the existence of a higher law. And when that higher law conflicts with man-made law, it is not only okay for a person to disobey the man-made law – it is his duty!

Of course, one's belief in the importance of the rule of law means that you also are duty-bound to suffer the consequences of breaking that law. And all of that is exactly what Rosa Parks did. She saw the higher law, broke the man-made law and went to jail for it willingly. What could possibly be wrong with that? A heroine.

On the other hand, what if I perceive that the higher law (presumably God's) says that there should be no abortions? Even though the man-made law says they're allowed. Am I therefore justified in killing doctors, nurses, receptionists and pregnant women at clinics? Well, I guess to be totally consistent I should say as long as I'm willing to face the legal music afterward. The trick for the anti-abortionist, I suppose, is to bomb an abortion clinic in a state that has outlawed the death penalty.

It's all too tough a call for me, though I, like you, cannot withhold my admiration for the profound and yet quiet courage of Rosa Parks.

But let me ask you something: we grew up in Detroit where Rosa Parks lived the last portion of her life, but were you aware of her? I never remember hearing her story until sometime after I left Detroit. Although I did hear it well before Aaron Neville sang it to me. You?

Terry.

✟   ✟   ✟

26 October 2005
Gilbert

Terry,

No, I never knew Rosa Parks lived in Detroit. Did she ever spend time with Bob Seger, Kid Rock or Eminem? There I go joking again about this great lady. But, I tell you, you should have heard her in that talk she gave, she was a happy woman. I loved that. She would not have minded.

Steve

27 October 2005 – New York, NY

steve

This one falls into the category of: "Who keeps tabs on these guys?"

Sig Frolich. Probably not a name you would recognize right off. Probably not even with a great deal of probing. But Sig, who died recently and got a two-column (!) obit in the *Globe and Mail*, was the last living of the 13 actors who played the flying monkeys in the *Wizard of Oz*. (10 points if you can name all of the other 12 – and their social security numbers, without notes.) Sig was the one who snatches Toto in the film.

Later in life he became a close personal friend of Mickey Rooney. Is this something one admits in public? Still, Sig carried on until the age of 97. Until just a few months ago he was signing autographs for visitors to his nursing home.

———

Sig's, of course, is the kind of show-biz immortality I am chasing by getting into the playwright game. Last night, as you may recall, was the premiere performance of my play, *Hamlet - The Sequel*. As you know, I had some doubts about how the whole thing would come off. To spoil the punch line – it was spectacular!

Miranda and I took the train up to Bridgeport in the morning. At noon, the director started taking the actors through a rough read-through and directed some staging as we went. My initial impression as we went through this was that the male lead was terrific and so was the supporting actress; I thought the female lead was … adequate. This first run-through took almost three and a half hours.

There was a break. And then the actors did a speed read through the play. Another break for dinner. And then the performance at seven-thirty.

I've been to quite a few play readings and my expectations were based on these experiences. Usually, the actors merely sit in chairs in a row across the stage and read their parts. But this was much more of a staged reading. The actors played out their parts as if this were a real performance. They moved; they kissed; they fought. The only thing that made it a reading was that they were holding their scripts as they went through the action.

The other thing was that I had expected a total audience of maybe 15 – all friends and relatives. In fact, thanks to some publicity in the Connecticut edition of the *New York Times*, there were about 70-80 people on hand. This was especially important I thought because the play is a comedy. People don't like to laugh alone.

The actual reading went off wonderfully. People got caught up in the characters and the plot; they laughed and responded with huge applause at the end. Maybe the biggest surprise to me was the lead actress who, I thought, was the star of the show. She had me on the verge of tears with her final soliloquy (and I knew what she was going to say). It just shows you how people work differently. Obviously during the initial read-through she was just feeling her way into the role, sorting it out. She saved her performance for the performance.

Afterwards I got up on stage and heard comments from the audience. It was supposed to be a feedback session, but wound up, rather gratifyingly, being a series of raves. These were from people I didn't know. All in all, a wonderful evening. There is even talk of having another reading later this year and possibly a full performance run next year.

All kinda heady.

t.

27 Oct. 2005
Gilbert

Dear Ter,

Now I really wish I'd been there! You have a "touch" that so many other writers don't have and that's a feel for what the average person would enjoy. That's why I keep trying to get you to read Tom Wolfe's last two books, *A Man In Full* and *Charlotte Simmons*. Because he has that same touch. Many times I could see this in your writing, but I don't think you yourself trusted it. Now, to have such a wonderful evening in the theater confirm it for you is a great thing and my hope is that it keeps you writing till your dying day. (Which I hope is not soon. I'm sure we both thought of the irony of one of us passing away during the writing of this book. Ironic, but not an ideal scene.)

s.

28.OCT.05 – NYC

steve.

One last thing before I leave August Wilson. In his obituary, he is quoted as saying that as a young man he used to haunt the Pittsburgh thrift shops and one day he picked up an old 78 of a song called "Nobody in Town Can Bake A Sweet Jelly Roll Like Mine." It was by a singer he'd never heard of before – Bessie Smith. Discovering that music, he said, was a turning point in his life. He said it was like the first record he had ever bought in his life – he suddenly knew what he was about.

If I die, I want you to set the record straight and tell the world that that the very first record I ever bought was a 45 called "I Love Mickey" sung by Teresa Brewer. To be honest (and in my obituary I guess you probably should be), it didn't change my life. I'd rather be able to say my first record was an Elvis record or Johnny Cash or Little Richard. But no, it was a stupid novelty song about Mickey Mantle! (He actually had a spoken line at the end of the record.) Do you remember Teresa? The hit of hers I remember best was called "Sweet Old-Fashioned Girl." I read a couple of years ago that she still sings professionally – but she sings jazz now.

t.

30October 2005
gilbert az.

terry,

I can identify with the angry black playwright Wilson. I'm not saying I'm black, because you may know I'm not. But my experience was similar (because all men are brothers). I remember buying my first Pat Boone record, and taking it home and playing it. It was right then that I knew what I was about.

I prefer humor over anger, when done well. Because humor takes more courage and creativity. That's why I admire your play, *Hamlet - The Sequel*, more than the angry plays of Wilson. It's easy to be angry. It's easy to feel Bessie Smith's pain and then eagerly grasp it as one's own.

I saw a very touching TV special recently on Mickey Mantle's life. I actually wept in parts. It was that well done. (But, then, I also wept during a special on the 9/11 World Series that the Arizona Diamondbacks, with whom I had over-identified, won over the Yankees.)

In a way, you were searching for a hero in your first record purchase. Joseph Campbell, the brilliant mythology scholar, would love that about you. Some day I will make the case that for you to seek a little piece of Mickey Mantle through Teresa Brewer was nobler than someone grasping on to the suffering in the voice of Bessie Smith. I'll be vilified by the *New York Times* and the *Village Voice*. But I'll be right.

Steve.

31 October 2005

steve

Obit today for Al Lopez. The guy was 97. He managed two very interesting teams to American League pennants – the 1954 Indians and the 1959 White Sox. From 1949 to 1964, the Yankees under Casey Stengel won the AL pennant every year but two – the two Lopez teams.

The '54 Indians set the major league record for wins – 111 wins in a 154 game season. The '59 Pale Hose were the famous Go-Go White Sox. When you write about sports a bit, you realize why sportswriters have to come up with these wild and cutesy nicknames for teams – otherwise you just wind up, as I would have in that last sentence, using "White Sox" twice in the space of 10 words. (Are the Diamondbacks sometimes called "the Snakes" I wonder, as in: SNAKES TOP TRIBE!)

Which pitchers led those Lopez teams in wins? (Hint: it's the same pitcher both times.)

t.

nov. 2 2005
gilbert

ter

Yes, our baseball team IS often called the Snakes, and, even more often the D-Backs. Diamondbacks is a long name, and sportswriters are short on time. It takes a lot of keystrokes to type out: Diamondbacks.

As to your quiz I'm going to guess Bob Lemon.

Now, about Al Lopez. It is a wonderful phenomenon to me that great coaches and great managers are almost never great players.

Almost never. And my theory on this is that if you have to struggle to learn something, like baseball, you are better at teaching it and coaching it. Al Lopez broke into the major leagues in 1928, and he played a lot of years and his batting average was .261. Not great. But he was a great manager.

I myself, part of the time, make my living as something they now call a "life coach." Some of my clients who have used other coaches say I am the best they've ever experienced. Modestly, I think they are probably correct. But one of the reasons why I have learned to coach it well is because I was so lousy for so many years at actually doing it. (Living.)

s.

✠   ✠   ✠

nov3-05 – LA, CA.

Steve.

Here in LA for Nick *[my nephew, Nicolas Hill. tnh]* and Danya's wedding obviously. And I guess I'll be seeing you at that event day after tomorrow. You're getting in tonight? Anyway, to more pressing matters:

Bob Lemon is wrong. Well, not really totally. You see, on the 1954 Indians, two pitchers tied for the team lead in wins with 23. One was Bob Lemon, but the other was Early Wynn. Early then won 22 to lead the White Sox to the pennant in 1959.

On the great-managers-are-almost-never-great-players thing. You better hope that Wayne Gretzsky proves to be the exception to the rule. Have you ever taken Kathy to an NHL hockey game? I took Miranda to her first game when we first started going out and, to my surprise, she took to it immediately. Since then I am instructed to get tickets to two or three Rangers games every year. Mark Messier was her favorite player.

t.

4 Nov. 2005
Gilbert

Terry,

Kathy and I love going to Diamondbacks games, usually with my son Bobby and her friend Deb. Kathy enjoys sports, and really enjoyed Big Ten hockey when she attended the University of Wisconsin. I told her that you and I, as boys, used to love Big Ten hockey as well, going up to Ann Arbor to see Michigan play. Kathy went to Wisconsin and I went to the University of Arizona, and I always like to note that these two colleges are almost always in Playboy's Top Ten Party Schools. It's good that Kathy and I never had a child together, it would have been Robert Downey, Jr.

Steve

9 noviembre 2005 – San Miguel de Allende, Guanajuato, Mexico

steve,

It was great to see you at Nick's wedding. Sorry we didn't get a chance to really talk except a bit at dinner, but those things are so socially demanding. For me anyway.

The day after (Sunday) we went to a post-wedding brunch on the corner of Hell and Gone and then came back and watched a bit of football before going out to a farewell dinner with Eunice and Jeff at a place just on the other side of Nowhere. I know it's a cliché, but LA seems so distressingly spread out to me. I'm used to living in cities (New York, Toronto, Paris, London, even here in San Miguel) where you can walk to restaurants for dinner or to a café for a cup of coffee or just to get the paper. All of those things require a car trip, a tank of gas, maps, parking and generally a lot of hassle in LA.

⌐══════╕

Anyway, the next morning we flew to Mexico. Arrived in Leon early afternoon and then were driven by our maid's husband an hour and a half to our home here. I think I've told you this, but we bought the house in April, went to NYC for May and then came back here in June. In June we got a lot of furniture and books moved down here that had been in storage for nine years.

We also had talks during our June stay with the builder, Gerardo – who had become a friend of ours by then – and agreed to have some additional work done. We had a studio for Miranda built on our roof and we added a covered patio off the living room in the front.

So when we arrived here in the late afternoon on Monday it was really the first look at all the work. We immediately did a once-around and on the whole were very pleased. But strangely, a number of things were left undone. I say "strangely" because when we last heard from Gerardo in early August, he said in an e-mail that the job was finished except for a few small things that he'd make sure were done in the next week – long before we were going to be back.

For instance, Miranda's studio was finished but there was no glass in the windows and three of the four walls were essentially nothing but windows. Also there were three ceiling fans that were supposed to be installed; there were none. And a number of other smaller things.

Yesterday we tried to call him on his cell. The message was that his phone was no longer in operation. No problem; Gerardo owns three shops in town and goes to each of them at some point during the day. So today we went to one of them and asked if Gerardo was in. The Mexican girl at the shop got a strange look on her face and said something I didn't understand. Well, this is a correspondence about death, so you've figured what's coming.

Gerardo was killed in a car accident near Mexico City on August 15th. He was 49. His mother and sister had been up from the capital for the weekend and he was driving them home. They were killed also. The only reason his wife, Mercedes, was not in the car was that she had a doctor's appointment the next day and had stayed in San Miguel.

But the reality is that death is a fact of life here in San Miguel. A constant presence. I've already told you about our Super Bowl Party experiences. And every week or so you see a funeral procession through the streets of the town with the casket in a car leading family and friends walking slowly behind. They walk all the way to the cemetery which is just outside of town. On my daily morning walk I pass two casket making shops.

Of course, this is the country – as you pointed out when we started this adventure – that celebrates the Day of the Dead. Our maid, Concepcion, told us that on the day, families take the deceased's favorite food, drink, cigarettes, etc. out to their graves and spend the night there. She said that naturally afterwards they take the food home and eat it themselves. But she told us seriously, "It has no taste," the spirit of the deceased having consumed it during the night.

I'd like a bag of Ruffles potato chips and a bottle of Sam Adams please. I wonder if it would be okay for you to drink the Sam Adams after the night. After all, my spirit would have consumed all the alcohol.

t.

11 NOV gilbert

ter,

So Gerardo is dead. And your house suffers. Can you find his actual obituary? After all, we are two guys who read the obituaries. And you wonder if I can drink the beer, being the alcoholic that I am...or, might we better say, recovered alcoholic that I am. After all, it is 27 years since I had a drink. Many people like to call themselves "recovering alcoholics" even after 27 years. I prefer to say "recovered."

In the 12-step program I used for my recovery one of the promises was that if we followed certain steps we would recover. It did not say that we would "always be recovering." It said we would recover. So I have recovered. I would say. But I better not say that in a meeting I might go to with Matt Scudder in New York when I see you there in May. Because if I do, the Correct-Phrase-Police in the AA meeting will come down on me. I'll drink the Sam Adams. That's a promise. So you better not die.

steve.

12 november 2005 – San Miguel de Allende, GTO, MX

Steve.

Down here, the daily English-language paper is the Mexican edition of the *Miami Herald*. And today the news is bad for Steve Courson. Dead at 50.

Ordinarily I wouldn't pay any attention to the obituary of a former Pittsburgh Steeler offensive lineman, but this one was odd.

He died when a tree he was cutting down – a big one: 44 feet high and 5 feet around – fell on him. Apparently he was trying to save his dog from the falling tree but wasn't quite quick enough. The dog, by the way was merely injured and taken to a vet. No such luck for Steve.

I see several lessons here. First, do not value your dog's life more than your own. Second, leave the tree chopping to the professionals! In decades of reading obits, I've yet to come across the notice of a lumberjack who died in the line of duty. Seems pretty clear to me: these guys know what they're doing – we don't.

A question: this obit got a 4-column heading, a picture and about 400 words on the front sports page of the *Herald*; was it even covered in the Phoenix paper? Or the *NYTimes*? (What *is* the Phoenix paper, by the way?)

Let me say that our house has not really suffered, thanks mainly to Gerardo's wife, who has bent over backward and berated various laborers to get work on the house done. Every time I suggest that maybe we don't need this or that, she refuses to compromise. "Gerardo is looking down on us," she says.

She's a remarkable woman who has a graduate degree in history and is still involved in the academic world in Mexico City, but now lives here and has had to take over the full running of the stores. Very capable, bright and attractive to boot.

I might check for an obit down here, but I'd have to go to some archive to get back to an August issue of the paper.

Terry.

14 Nov. 2005 PHOENIX

terry

The Phoenix paper is *The Arizona Republic* (or the *Mesa Tribune*) but no one reads these papers anymore...like me, they get all their news from their favorite websites each morning and their analysis from their favorite blogs...more timely, more intelligent, more sane than the newspapers are.

The *NYTimes* did have Courson's death featured but the main focus was not the tree that felled him but rather the steroids he admitted to taking. His life after football was devoted to speaking out against steroid use. Then a tree falls on him. Poor guy. But he did save the dog. In Kathy's eyes he did the right thing. She is such an animal person that she puts them ahead of humans on the great chain of being, the great Mandala, the circle of life. I only rate because she once looked at me from a certain angle and thought I had "basset hound eyes." True, my eyes are sad a lot. But that's because my favorite teams are almost always losing. Unlike the hyped up Steelers with Courson and his fellow Injectors.

Steve.

27 November 2005 – San Miguel de Allende, GTO, MX

Steve.

While we were living in England I began to become a bit of a soccer fan. Of course, this last sentence would sound ludicrous to anyone in England where the game is called, for good reason, "football." I say "for good reason" to distinguish it from our "football" which has not much to do with feet at all.

I was not really a total stranger to soccer when I moved to the UK. While in Toronto at Grey Advertising, I handled the advertising for the Toronto Blizzard, Toronto's entry in the North American Soccer League. With Toronto's ethnic make-up, the team should have been a success, but it wasn't; average attendance was probably under 5000 a game. (Perhaps the advertising was bad.) I think the team only survived maybe three years. However, while it was around I had access to a press box seat at all the games – a perk I took advantage of, seeing maybe six or seven games a season. After watching a few matches you get familiar enough with the game to understand the basic rules, which are much simpler than any North American sport, and you get a sense of when an offensive play is dangerous and what the players are trying to set up.

In London we lived in South Kensington within easy walking distance of Stamford Bridge, the Chelsea Stadium, so I kind of became a Chelsea fan. But you also become a fan of the English national team and, almost by default during those years, a Manchester United ("Man U") fan. The reason for this last is that during the years we were there, Manchester United always won the Premier Division and the top three teams in that Division got to participate in the European tournaments which were very exciting and always on television so, wanting to root for an English team, you'd root for Man U because they were usually the most successful UK team in these tournaments.

In fact, within England Man U is seen much as the Yankees are seen here. They are either loved or hated and there are many supporters of other teams that want nothing more than to see Man U beaten every week. Still these same English Man U haters will root for them in the international tournaments when they are playing Real Madrid or Inter Milan, for instance. After all, Man U *is* an English team.

All of this in aid of getting to the death the day before yesterday of George Best at 59. In his early twenties he was without a doubt England's top player. And he was perhaps the man who had the most to do with Manchester United's legendary status. How important he was is indicated by the fact that English Prime Minister Tony Blair commented on his death, calling him "the most naturally gifted player of his generation."

He lived a rock star lifestyle and was pretty generally unsuccessful in his battle with alcoholism. He was once quoted as saying, "I spent a lot of money on booze, birds and fast cars. The rest I just squandered." This pace obviously had a lot to do with his early death which was from multiple organ failure, including a liver which had started its existence as somebody else's.

All of this I am aware of not because he was a star while I was in the country, but because you'd hear of him the way you'd hear of Babe Ruth or Joe DiMaggio if you became a baseball fan now in the US. But, alright, here's the fact in the obit that I didn't know and one of the things that makes soccer such a great and universally loved and played game around the world: Best was only 5-foot-5.

It's a game ordinary-sized human beings can play.

t.

29 November 2005
Gilbert, AZ.

Terry,

I myself am not a soccer fan. You can't use your arms or hands? I'm not watching that.

Steve

30NOV2005 – San Miguel

Steve.

Did you notice Vic Power died yesterday? I close my eyes and I can picture two of his baseball cards from his playing (and my collecting) days. I also remember what they confirm in the *NYT* obit – that he was a great fielder. Moose Skowron said Power covered more ground than any other first baseman because he played fifteen feet further back than any other first baseman. He'd catch the throws at first base on the dead run, Skowron claimed.

There was some announcer – Van Patrick? probably – who always used to call him "Powers." It drove my father nuts.

t.

PHX 1dec. 2005

ter

As to the announcer calling Vic Power "Powers," perhaps it was a subconscious tribute. Stupid people often communicate subconsciously. Perhaps Mr. Patrick thought Vic could do SO many things, had so many powers.

But could he hit? I looked it up after I got your letter today. He had seasons of .319, .312 and .309 with a lifetime of .282. Not bad. But ironically he had no power. 19 was his top home run year, and for a first baseman that's not ideal. And maybe not all that ironic, because his name wasn't really Power. It was *Victor Felipe Pellot Pove*. Why would he name himself Power? Wouldn't that just disappoint the scouts? Why not Victor Glover? He was Puerto Rican, although from his baseball card we took him to be an African-American. He was a four-time all-star and seven-time gold glove winner for his fielding. A lot of good memories flow back when I think of him. I pray he will rest in peace.

s.

1DEC2005 – SMA, GTO, MX

Steve.

Yes, I looked up Power's record, too. One of the really interesting, and odd, things about his record was that in one game (against the Detroit Tigers, by the way) he stole home *twice*, including the game winner in extra innings. What made the incident weird to me was the fact that in that entire season he only stole a *total* of 3 bases!

t.

3 Dec 2005
PHX

terry

If a guy steals home early in the game, you think they would keep an extra eye on him the next time he reaches third base. Now I have to picture the Tigers all slapping their foreheads when he steals the game-winner.

Steve

4DEC2005 – San Miguel de Allende, GTO, MX

Steve,

I was in the midst of reading the draft of your little novel, *The Small Business Millionaire*, when I came across the obituary of Franz Jolowicz in *The New York Times* (on-line). Be sure and note it, though it flies in the face of much of what you say in the book.

Jolowicz ran for years and later owned the Discophile record store in Greenwich Village. The *Times* described the store in the early eighties as "possibly the finest record store in the world." You'd think such a store would be able to stay in business, wouldn't you? The place closed its doors in 1984 – forced out of business by a nearby Towers that opened just before that.

I didn't know the Discophile (I moved to the city at the beginning of 1985, the year after it closed) and the fact is I probably wouldn't have paid that much attention to it even if I had been in New York while it was around because its big specialty was classical music. And while I'll buy a classical album occasionally, I'd hardly seek out a specialty store for it.

However, I do know and shop at the big, bad Tower (which is still there) all the time. We can gnash our teeth and moan about the disappearance of the small specialty shops – the book and record stores, etc. of our memory (and I do it often), but the fact is those big, bad chain places are often pretty good. That Tower advertises itself as open 364 days a year; it's convenient; it has a great selection in stock; and it even has a few people working there that know and care about the music. Whenever I go there – usually to buy a specific CD – I generally walk out with somewhere between $50 and $100 worth of music.

I'm sure I would have loved Discophile (or a similar shop specializing in folk or country music) and would have mourned its demise. But I'd sure hate to give up Tower. Ironically, now those big chain stores are in their own danger because of people taking to getting their music off the internet.

It's our choice: we can either rail against change or accommodate it. Since change is well-known to be inevitable, I'll go with the latter option.

t.

6 December 2005

Ter,

Actually I don't think *The Small Business Millionaire* protagonist, Jonathan, would disagree with you at all. He would shop at Tower if he could find more and better music there. However, if he took on Discophile as a consulting client, he would show them how to thrive in the face of the challenge. If they really wanted to. Sometimes little stores, like Meg Ryan's bookstore in *You've Got Mail*, are ready to cave. They've had enough. So they'll use the behemoth as their story. (As in "forced out of business." No one is forced out of business. It's a story.)

I agree with your observations about change. Darwin said it wasn't the strongest that survived, but rather those who could adapt best. Like Matt Leinart, the quarterback of University of Southern California this year in what was, I believe, the best football game I have ever seen on TV when USC just barely beat Notre Dame because Leinart kept changing and adapting and being open to anything. Tom Brady is good at that, too. You've got your big strong quarterbacks like Ryan Leaf who don't make it, and then those that Darwin would love.

Link Wray died a week ago. I read about it in *Rolling Stone* while flying from Columbus, Ohio, to Phoenix today. Link was quite an innovative guitarist in his time. Remember "Rumble"? One of the first and best guitar hit singles back when we were teens. In a recent concert Dylan did a cover of "Rumble" to honor the passing of Link Wray. One time Link Wray went into a studio where the Who were recording and Pete Townshend got down on his knees to Link, literally, saying he was the one that started rock and roll guitar. He played guitar right up to the end, dying at 76 in the middle of a tour. I love that. I read about a writer once in Elizabethan times who on his death bed pantomimed writing with his hands and then died. I loved that. I want to die that way. Not soon. But that way.

s.

10DEC2005 – San Miguel de Allende, GTO, MX

Steve.

So I've just been to a dinner party at the home of a guy here who knows I have an unnatural interest in the obituaries and death. "Oh, just before you got here," he said, "I was on the internet and you'll be happy to know that Richard Pryor and Eugene McCarthy died today."

"That's interesting," I said, "but we really try to write only about people who die this year." You see, I was under the mistaken impression that both Pryor and McCarthy were already some years dead and that what he was telling me was that this was the anniversary of their deaths.

Okay, so now I'm going to have to readjust my thinking: Pryor and McCarthy are dead AGAIN! Really, this time.

On reflection I realize that I have never been able to sort out the difference between Richard Pryor and Freddie Prinze. (Now, Freddie *is* dead, isn't he?)

This is all rather embarrassing since the obvious reason for the Prinze/Pryor confusion is that they are both comedians and their last names both begin with Ps. I can think of no other possible reason for my confusion. I just hate to admit that all comedians with last names starting with P look the same to me.

McCarthy, on the other hand, I have no convenient excuse for thinking he was already dead. He was kind of a hero of mine. A man who, I used to say, single-handedly stopped a war. This was clearly an overly-dramatic interpretation of events on my part.

History will note that McCarthy's standing up to be counted on his opposition to the war was in 1968, while the war didn't end (at least as far as the US was concerned) until 1974. But at the time, his open opposition to the war and his Presidential candidacy said to me that all the anti-Viet Nam War protests actually had an effect, that someone in the establishment (and what could be more establishment than the US Senate?) was actually paying attention and didn't merely dismiss the dissent as a few bleeding-heart pacifist fag malcontents.

In the end, of course, he didn't really have the "want-to" to be President. And his campaign showed it. Had I been given the chance, even I would have voted for Bobby over Gene as much as I admired McCarthy for running in the primaries against a sitting President. In some ways it could be said, I suppose, that he died in 1968, at least as a serious political figure.

In some law of all things it is written that politicians have to be serious human beings. At least if they want to get elected. This is too bad because it means they aren't allowed to exhibit any real sense of humor or see any issue in any other color than either black or white.

The truths are that 99.9% of all issues are gray and that the world is a cosmic joke.

By having a system that says the only people who can get elected to office are those who refuse to acknowledge these truths means we wind up with a group of people running our governments who are totally outside of reality. These people play their own game by a set of rules that doesn't much matter to the rest of us. I do not believe that the central motivating force of any person who goes into "public service" should be: Get Elected at any cost. But it is.

Why do you think Hillary Clinton voted for the War on Iraq? Why do you think she's trying to explain away that vote now? You don't need a weatherman to know which way the wind blows; you just need a Gallup poll. Gene McCarthy didn't need a poll. Of course, he never got to be President either.

Still, he unseated one.

t.

10dec2005 – gilbert az

dear ter

Nice job summarizing Gene McCarthy. I remember his courage and wit, too, and I remember supporting him enthusiastically, and loving the fact that he was also a good poet! A poet politician! Poland has playwright-politicians, why not? I share your admiration for what he did. I share your loathing for people who want to be president (or anything else) just to get elected. He was not one of those. I remember being almost physically ill when reading George Stephanopoulos's account of what happened after Bill Clinton got elected and they (his team) all woke up without a purpose, their sole purpose (electing Bill) having been accomplished. Then, Stephanopoulos said, "it finally occurred to us what our purpose and mission would be for the first four years in office: to get re-elected!" That's the snake consuming its tail.

I don't share your lumping Richard Pryor with Freddie Prinze, though! Dude! Richard Pryor was absolutely hilarious over and over again in concert and in his movies whereas poor Freddie Prinze, funny though he was, in a low key way, was so "over before he began," having had just a TV show then out on a drug overdose. *Chico and the Man*! So Freddie was a funny Hispanic, and Richard Pryor was, by his own bestselling album of the same name, a "crazy nigger!" (his words) who turned race on its head with really groundbreaking humor. He made Eddie Murphy and Chris Rock who they are ... but I think I've always followed comedy more closely than you, trying, of course, to steal as much as I can as I go. Given that I have to give a lot of talks for a living. I remember your father first turning me on to the very concept of the comedy album. Listening to Allan Sherman, Bob Newhart and Stan Freberg. That was in the 50s. Later, Pryor's comedy albums broke all kinds of records, and he was amazing in his live concert albums. Now he's dead, rather amazing that he lived to 63, given all the self-abuse and then contracting MS later in life.

Speaking of how long people live, it hit me today, reading some older obituaries. Our title is *Two Guys Read the Obituaries*; it doesn't say from what era, although we've agreed to keep our writing about 2005, soon to be over, but you know how the *NYTimes* obit section on the internet runs old obits, too, for the fun of it? Well I read some older ones today, and noticed that both F. Scott Fitzgerald and Elvis died in their early 40s, E. at 42 and F.S. at 44, and that Roger Maris, who died at 51, was born in the same little Minnesota town (Hibbing) that Bob Dylan was born in. This world of ours is just one small family after all. One little Mister Rogers' neighborhood out there in right field, Yankee Stadium. And every time I get a cold and see the obits that morning and see someone 61 dead I think I'm dead! Maybe this is it!

Steve.

12DEC2005-SMA, GTO, MX

Steve.

You're right when you suggest that you kept/keep more up on the world of intentional comedy than I. I specialize more in unintentional comedy. My reason for the Prinze/Pryor confusion is that I'd only heard of them. I don't believe I ever actually saw either of them perform their acts – though I did see Richard Pryor in an only fair movie called *Silver Streak* co-starring Gene Wilder.

(The main thing I remember about the film was that it all took place on a train trip from Los Angeles to Chicago. When the train left the station early in the movie, there was a shot of the retreating "LA" skyline in which clearly visible was the CN Tower – then a brand new Toronto landmark and clearly recognizable by any Torontonian, which I was at the time. When the train dramatically arrives in Chicago, that same Torontonian would recognize the terminal as Union Station in Toronto. Now, of course, all films are shot in Toronto so everyone believes that the CN Tower is actually located in either LA or New York.)

I had almost forgotten those comedy albums my parents used to play all the time in the late '50s and early '60s. And yet many of the lines from those albums – especially from Freberg and Newhart – are family touchstones now. Those routines are so well known to us that they're often quoted when we get together. My parents must have played them a lot. They were also big Bob&Ray fans. I wonder how any of that stuff would hold up today.

I might add that in your mention of the comedy albums my parents used to have you forgot Shelley Berman.

btw (as they say in e-mail-speak). Wasn't it Czechoslovakia that had a playwright-politician – not Poland? Or are there also Polish playwright-politicians that I simply haven't kept up on, in the same way I haven't really kept up with comedy?

And finally, in connection with my comment, and belief, that politicians with a sense of humor are unelectable, I bumped into this Ambrose Bierce quote on the internet yesterday: "Ability is commonly found to consist mainly in a high degree of solemnity."

Ambrose himself couldn't have gotten himself elected to a PTA Board. He's probably laughing now somewhere, no doubt hanging out with Amelia Earhart.

t.

13 dec 2005
gilbert az

terry

To make your point again, Morris Udall of Arizona, a bright politician often mentioned as presidential material, was finally declared, as his biography was titled, "Too Funny to be President."

I didn't forget Shelley Berman. He is my all-time favorite for comedy albums from that era. In fact what a delight to see him now on *Curb Your Enthusiasm* as Larry David's father, and still amazingly hilarious. I just couldn't remember if your folks had him in their collections, too. Yes, those albums, and humor itself was a major part of your parents' life for which I am forever grateful. It was a big influence on me and who knows without it I may have gone on to take life seriously. That would have been a tragedy for a lot of people.

s.

14DEC2005 – SMA

Steve.

In the first place, I don't think you ever would have taken life seriously – you're far too intelligent for that.

In the second place: SHELLEY BERMAN'S ON THE LARRY DAVID SHOW!!! I didn't know that. On the other hand, and this gets back to my not keeping up with intentional humor, I've never seen *Curb Your Enthusiasm*. I don't even know the set-up. So, of course, I didn't realize that Larry David had a father. (Well, I mean I knew it in the *abstract*. I just didn't know it in the context of the show.)

You'd think, actually, that I would have made a point of watching the show since I have twice in New York been stalked (okay, in a minor way) – and confronted – by people who were under the impression I *WAS* Larry David. I've seen pictures of the guy and I personally don't see the similarity – I mean the guy *is* bald, for chrissake.

The last time I saw Shelley Berman was in a quite wonderful movie about politics based on a play by Gore Vidal. It was called *The Best Man*. Berman had a small but crucial role which I thought he played brilliantly. That must have been 1964 or '65. After that – for the next forty-plus years – I never heard of him again until your note yesterday.

As a postscript, I saw *The Best Man* as a play on Broadway four or five years ago and still thought it was terrific, but I thought Berman did a better job than the Broadway actor who played his role.

t.

20 December 2005

ter

   I notice in yesterday's obituaries that former NFL Pro Bowl lineman Darrell Russell was killed in a high-speed car crash. He was 29. Rarely do you get the kind of detailed playback, in an obituary, of the actual crash. Imagine his family, in years to come, opening their scrapbook and reading that Darrell's car, being driven by former teammate and co-fatality Mike Bastianelli, "went out of control about 6 a.m. and hit a curb, a tree, a newsstand, a fire hydrant, a light pole, another tree and an unoccupied transit bus." They will picture that sequence forever. The obit adds, for context, that Darrell had never quite beaten his drug problems. In an attempt to end the obit on a positive note, the *Times* finished it up (for the family's future reading) this way: "In September 2002, prosecutors dropped rape charges against Russell, claiming they could not prove he videotaped a woman being raped by two of his friends in January 2002."

   Hey, Ter, as you and I wind up our writing of this obituary book I notice that our first book written together (*Two Guys Read Moby-Dick*) and due out in a month or so, is already selling well on Amazon, having jumped from the millions in rankings to one of the top 25,000 bestsellers. (There are about two million active titles for sale on Amazon.) That's pretty amazing for a book that hasn't been released yet. Do you know of any people who might have made mass purchases? I can think of two, but on reflection I realize that both your mother and mine are dead.

S

23dec2005 – sma

s.

yes, I know of about six people who've bought (or ordered) the book on Amazon.com and one person who ordered from Borders.com. Obviously my little personal marketing plan has moved us up in the rankings about a million places. This is much more successful than we were at getting "The Mosey" in the top ten on Bob Terry's Hi-Beat show.

t

[Note: When Steve and I were in Jr. High School we invented a non-existent song called "The Mosey." (This was at the time of a hit – and corresponding dance – called "The Stroll.") We then tried to get it ranked in the top-ten on a show – Bob Terry's Hi-Beat – which claimed they based their top-ten (played every Friday) on the number of requests they received. We called in with our requests for this mythical song time and time again, but it never made it into the top ten. Of course, what would they have played if it had made it? tnh]

23dec2005 – ph, az

t.

Your mention of that old Detroit disc jockey from the 50's, Bob Terry, made me wonder whether maybe he had died this year. So I went in search of an obit for him.

Here's what I found!

Bob "Nighthawk" Terry was on the air in Washington DC in the 70s from 7-11PM, swilling Coke from a can to make it sound like he was drinking his sponsor's

National Beer. He disappeared from a concert that he, and some investors, put on at the Take-It-Easy Ranch in southern Maryland. Along with Bob, over $200,000 in gate receipts also disappeared.

His Oldsmobile was later found, burned out, with a man behind the wheel, in a swamp in North Carolina. The ONLY way to identify the corpse was by the set of false teeth found in the car. They matched Nighthawk's denture pattern. Those who know him well do not believe that was Nighthawk in the car and suspect that he put a "patsy" in there with his teeth. "Hawk" was a shrewd, scary kind of guy with some serious friends.

S.

23DEC2005 – sma, mx

s.

Now seriously, is that the same Bob Terry that we knew from late 1950s morning radio in Detroit? Did you find any more in his bio to suggest that?

Anyway to answer your earlier question, yes Bob Terry is alive and was seen only last year with Amelia Earhart (she looks awful, by the way), Captain Noonan and Ambrose Bierce. They were playing bridge together. No need to tell you who Amelia's "partner" was. *[This last is a reference to a song Steve and I used to sing together. It was called "Amelia Earhart's Last Flight" and it featured the line "With her partner, Captain Noonan, on the second of July / Her plane fell in the ocean, far away." tnh.]*

t.

23 December 2005

Ter,

You and I used to sing that Amelia Earhart song and my little sister Cindy would often overhear us singing it. Later in her life Cindy took flying lessons and actually soloed, all because of her love and fascination with Amelia Earhart. (We could really deliver a song in those days....and will have an opportunity to prove we can once again as I'll bring my guitar with me in February when Kathy and I come to visit you in Mexico.)

S.

24 DEC 2005 – SMA, GTO, MX

steve.

There was an obit yesterday for the biochemist who invented light beer. The concept was produced by Rheingold Brewery in New York and then Meister Brau in Chicago before going to Miller Brewery which put all its marketing clout behind it and made a huge success of Miller Lite.

Okay, so maybe it wasn't the most important twentieth century invention, but surely anyone would put it in the top three or four. If it hadn't been for light beer I suspect that a very high percentage of American males would be overweight.

You know the immutable laws of weight loss/gain as well as I. And the bottom line is that 3500 calories equals 1 pound. Since light beers are generally 50 calories per bottle less than regular beer, you save a pound every 70 beers you drink. So all you have to do to keep in shape is put away ten beers a day and each week you'll lose a pound. That's right isn't it?

The other interesting thing about this guy's obit is that today the *Times* published a rather extended correction on his obit. There were four errors of fact in it. The original obit was only 420 words. Four errors! And unless I'm wrong, it appears to me there was also an error in the *correction*; I suppose tomorrow there will be a correction of the correction.

t.

24 dec 2005
gilbert

Dear Terry,

By the way Feliz Navidad down south there in Mexico.

The reason I wanted to send you that Bob Terry "possible obit" was to see if I can help liven up the conclusion of this exchange with a violent death, or even a faked death, at the very end. (Notice how death is said to "liven" things up? Death is known to be a great wake-up call for that.)

I didn't want this book to be like Simon and Garfunkel's song, "Old Friends." Where we just exchange musings about the dead like old friends who sit on the park bench like bookends.

I'd rather it be something wherein an old deejay that we once tried to reach on the phone and manipulate fakes his own death. Ironic! Maybe we gave him the idea! We faked a group called the Chesney Brothers and a song called "The Mosey," and maybe he filed that deceptive move away subconsciously. Maybe when we did that he said to himself, "I never realized that you could blur the line between reality and fiction like these lads have done." Then, later on, with all that money on the line, he fakes his death.

That is more the book I'd like my name on. One with that kind of story. Rather than the old friends/bookends talking to each other with the newspapers swirling in the eddies around their ankles on that park bench in Central Park.

s.

25 December 2005 – SMA, GTO, MX

steve.

Feliz Navidad!

I appreciate your panic about trying to make this book seem like something someone might want to read. Virtually every day I think "who would want to read this stuff?" And the problem is I can't come up with any names.

Not only that – here we are only seven days from the end of our artificially mandated year of obituaries and it seems to me that I haven't sorted out a lot of the things I wanted to sort out.

I did not enter this project with the high hopes you had. I had no dream of wanting to grapple with Death and wrestle that old humbug to a standstill – to take on the reaper and make him a weeper.

My goal was much more modest. I merely wanted to get some kind of a grip on our time through writing about some of the figures that populated it. Like most writers, I find that I often don't really know what I think until I try to write it. I thought trying to write about these people would help me sort out an era – my era. You suggest that we probably come across in this correspondence like two old geezers sitting on a park bench gradually dying of nostalgia.

Reliving old times was not my intent – understanding was.

And yet, so much remains a mystery. I still don't really know what I think about Viet Nam. I still don't know why I wasn't down in Mississippi in the early sixties registering voters and getting thrown in jail or killed. I am no closer to understanding how in 1961 Norm Cash was able to hit .361 with 41 home runs and 132 RBIs and score 119 runs when in 16 other big league seasons he was never once able to hit .300, hit 40 home runs, or drive in or score even 100 runs! This was before the age of steroids. Also the Nixon administration still baffles me.

So maybe, in the end, the book should be called *Two Geezers Read the Obituaries*, and we *are* just sitting on that park bench doing a sappy version of *This Is Your Life*.

(Can you imagine a *non-sappy* version of *This Is Your Life?*)

Speaking of which, neither of us remarked at the time on the death of Ralph Edwards, the show's host. He died in November at the age of 92. I have the obit from the *LA Times* in front of me and it says Edwards was still putting in time at his office as head of Ralph Edwards Productions when he was 90. It also says that when he first moved to New York in his 20s he "ate 10-cent meals and slept on park benches."

I wonder if he ever saw two old geezers in the park?

t.

26 December 2005
gilbert az

Dear Terry,

Same Navidad to you right back. I began my Christmas morning by firing off an angry letter to the editor of my local newspaper, the *Arizona Republic*. In it I cancelled my subscription. I can't recall the full text of the letter, because it was one of those violent screeds that you just tear out of your heart. But I was raging against the dying of the Christmas light. When I picked up the morning paper on Christmas morning, instead of the usual beautiful, colorful MERRY CHRISTMAS along the top of the front page, there was a very lame "Happy Holidays." You could barely see it.

So I tore off a letter raging at the paper for caving in to the most cowardly and sheepish herd-following known as political correctness, a movement based on fear of offending anyone who might be able to someday vote for your cause. The cowardice of that graceless fear-based tiptoeing enraged me. I would have preferred GOD IS DEAD! At least they would be being bold and authentic.

Newspapers themselves deserve an obituary this year because people can't stand how irrelevant the newspapers have become and how politically smug and imitative. What does the *New York Times* think of the Bush speech? Well, what a coincidence! That's what we ALL think! No one today in the mainstream newspapers or at cocktail parties is offering up an original thought. Can you blame people for preferring the internet blogs? For canceling their subscriptions? People are at cocktail parties to repeat things they've read in their dead paper or seen on CNN in the airport. This is one of the reasons I loathe almost all social occasions.

I enjoy close friends and family because the talk is more spontaneous and unguarded. You get the essence of the real person sitting beside you.

I heard Paul McCartney being interviewed a few days ago about 2006…the year he turns 64. His lighthearted Beatles song, "When I'm 64" was the topic and he said, "When you write something like that you never think it will actually happen to you." Indeed. And it was a young Paul Simon who wrote about the old friends sitting on the park bench like bookends. With this haunting little bridge:

> "Can you imagine us years from today,
> Sharing a park bench quietly
> How terribly strange to be seventy"

We went to see Dr. Andrew Weil the other night give a talk about aging. He said the ideal is to live at a wonderful clip and then when the decline comes have it be really rapid. BOOM! You're dead!

I want my obit to say that I did a few bold things. You ask yourself why you weren't there marching against racism. Why not do that today? When you and Miranda took that bus from New York to Washington to protest against the imminent Iraq war (which I was in favor of) why was that any less heroic? I truly believe that if there is one thing I want to say to my kids and my grandkids and anyone who reads a word I write, it's this: The opportunities to do heroic and important things are right here right now. Not in some better past or some more opportune future. Right now. The present moment rules.

March now. Write the great American novel now. Right now. The sense of linear time that those old friends on the park bench have is pure illusion.

Steve.

28DEC2005 (Alamo Bowl Tonight!) – San Miguel, GTO, MX

S.

As a man learning Spanish down here, I have strongly embraced your "the present moment rules" philosophy. My feeling is that what's past is past and needn't be spoken of anymore. And what's in the future … well, that's something no man can know for certain – so you only spit in fate's face by talking of it.

And this is my philosophical basis for always speaking Spanish in the present tense.

I also think it's interesting that you and I – from opposite sides of the political fence – have both, in these pages, expressed an open disgust for politics and the games politicians play while they're winking at each other. At their best, politicians are gutless jellyfish trying to stay afloat on the tide of public opinion. At their worst they combine this spinelessness with mendacity and common criminality. It makes me rather ill actually, but seriously what is one to do? The only people who run for office are – you guessed it – politicians. Opting out of the whole process by not voting doesn't solve anything; the process continues.

And yet, complaining about political game-playing doesn't solve anything either; the process continues.

I, as a registered New York Democrat, have twice written Hillary Clinton saying I will never vote for her again because of her eagerly-voted support of our invasion of Iraq. They obviously don't even bother to read what I write. (I would say that they probably don't even open the envelopes, but I'll make you a tiny wager that they open them enough to see if they contain checks.) I have never received a single shred of explanation for her stand – or her recantation – from her or her "handlers." Instead I have received a number of requests for money for her next campaign. The process continues … without me this time I'm afraid. I'm tired.

t.

gilbert az. 28 Dec. 2005

t.

Perhaps you might have possibly noticed that speaking Spanish only in the present tense is easier too! Still, I admire you for converting a shortcoming into something that enhances your character. A trick I've tried to perfect all my life. And speaking of tricks, I think if we've learned one thing during this whole year of reading obituaries, it is to understand what the trick to a great life is.

The trick is not to die. Or ever to be a bookend. Do you know who is not a bookend, sitting on the park bench? B.B. King. I just downloaded his latest album for my workouts and walks because I love the idea of being pushed onward by a man who is 80! He is 80 and this album totally rocks. His playing and singing are at their very peak!

Speaking of being in playing and singing trim, I'm glad to hear you are playing your new guitar in anticipation of my visit with mine. *[Steve and I had talked on the phone about the possibility of his coming down to San Miguel to do a reading for our first book* Two Guys Read Moby-Dick. *I told him that I'd bought a cheap guitar down here and was playing and singing a bit again. TNH]* Here is the playlist of the songs you and I performed in a bar when we were 19 (I still have the notebook dated August 20, 1963): "Take This Hammer," "Train Medley," "Rambler Gambler," "If I Had A Hammer," "Run Come See," "Jamaica Farewell," "Sloop John B," "Blowin' in the Wind," "Delia's Gone," "Down By The Riverside," "Hi Lili Hi Lo," "500 Miles," "Sister Sally," "Good News/Swing Low," "Brown Eyes," "This Land Is Your Land,"

"Gypsy Rover," "Abilene," "Whiskey in the Jar" and "Banks of the Ohio." Please brush up on all of them. I have lyrics and chords if you need them. It's only been 41 years so you probably don't.

s.

30dec05 – San Miguel

s.

For the life of me I cannot remember a song called "Run Come See." Did you do it solo? Maybe you had me just hum the harmony while you kept me in the dark as to what the name of the song was?

Meanwhile, I was casting about for a suitable final obit. Obviously if you or I had died during the last 365 it would have made a fitting artistic ending to the book for him who remained to write the other's obit. But as artistically "neat" as that would have been, I have to admit, I would not have been happy. The fact is I was openly rooting against that ending.

Anyway, when I think back on this year of obituaries it strikes me that the ones I liked reading most were not the major figures – Westmoreland, Arthur Miller, Gene McCarthy, Johnny Carson, Rosa Parks, etc. – but rather the lesser known who sneaked in for some reason or other. The guy in Quebec who hung with Mordecai Richler. Gene Baylos, the comedian who could make comedians laugh. The Civil War re-enactor. All people I'd never heard of before they died – and the obit told their story.

Maybe I liked these best because these people are closer in presence to me.

Anyway, I wanted somebody like that to end my part of this. On the day after Christmas, fate provided.

I think I've told you before what wonderful obits the London *Daily Telegraph* does – the paper's quite well-known for them in the UK. It was there I found Sandy Fawkes. A rather remarkable life even if not one I'd much like to live.

She was found as an infant in 1929 in the Grand Union Canal in England. Found! Now what does that mean? Was she floating down the canal? Was she swimming? The obit is shamefully lacking in this vital information. She was raised in a series of foster homes and never found out who her parents were.

Apparently she was bright and had a bit of artistic talent and got a scholarship to a good art school. She parlayed the art education into a job with a fashion magazine and moved into journalism from there.

Now – as if starting her life by being found in a canal weren't enough – her life gets strange. In 1974, in the US working briefly for the *National Enquirer*, she meets a man in a bar in Atlanta. Kinda falls for him. Packs it up and goes on the road with him for a week or so. Finds him just a bit too weird. Leaves him. A few days later, the police announce that they've caught a serial killer of 18 people named Paul Knowles, who turns out to be the same guy she'd run away with.

The police thought maybe she had been a part of the murders and pulled her in for questioning in Macon, GA. "Police in Macon, Georgia, make Rod Steiger look like a fairy," she later wrote. The whole thing shook her up a bit as she kept wondering why Knowles hadn't killed her too.

Anyway she returned to England and got very serious about her third and final profession – she became a drunk. From the facts in the obit, it appears she was rather famous for this role. It's the first obit I can remember of all the ones I've read over the years that actually named bars that the subject of the obituary frequented. (With Sandy the accent is on "frequent.") She hung out at the Coach and Horses pub and at the York Minster (aka The French Pub). Both are in the Soho area of London.

The obituary relates a number of amusing incidents from her last thirty years – all of them involved her drinking and all of them featured other well-known drunks. The one thing I've learned about drunks is they're much funnier to read about than to be with. So no, I'm not particularly sorry to have missed knowing her; but what an amazing basis for fame – being a drunk.

t.

31 December 2005 – gilbert

Terry,

Now, bring on 2006! Dick Clark is going to be LIVE on TV tonight from Times Square even though he's had a stroke and his speech will be odd. He is a warrior! (Or a vain fool who doesn't know when to quit, but often the difference is hard to determine.)

A final reflection on all these deaths we have written about. I've often heard it said that people long for eternity but wouldn't know what to do with an extra day if they were given it. One thing I've always treasured about our friendship, since the day it began in the 1950s, is that we always knew what to do with time together. There was always a game to get going or a project to create. So I'd like to leave you, and us, this year with my favorite Alan Watts quote about death and the games you and I played (and still play) called life:

"The world is a spell, an enchantment, an amazement, an arabesque of such stunning rhythm and a plot so intriguing that we are drawn by its web into a state of involvement where we forget that it is a game."

Be blessed in the coming year,

Steve

About the Authors

Both Steve Chandler and Terrence N. Hill have been writers all their lives. This book is the sequel to their critically-acclaimed Two Guys Read Moby-Dick.

Steve is the author of 13 popular books in the area of personal growth. His books have been translated into 15 languages. He is a celebrated speaker and has produced two award-winning audiobooks. Steve has also been the editor of a publishing house and a literary journal, a newspaper journalist and a songwriter. Steve's website is www.stevechandler.com, and you can email him at 100Ways@Compuserve.com.

Terry Hill worked for more than thirty years in advertising, beginning as a copywriter and later running agencies in New York and Europe. He has published poetry, essays and short fiction, and was the writer for two CBC-TV (Canada) documentary series. In 2005, Terry's first play, Hamlet - The Sequel, *won the Playhouse on the Green (Bridgeport, CT) playwriting competition. You can email Terry at terrynhill@hotmail.com.*